Kaplan Publishing are constantly ~~finding~~ ways to make a difference to your studies and our exciting online resources really do offer something different to students looking for exam success.

This book comes with free EN-gage online resources so that you can study anytime, anywhere.

Having purchased this book, you have access to the following online study materials:

CONTENT	ACCA (including FFA,FAB,FMA)		AAT		FIA (excluding FFA,FAB,FMA)	
	Text	Kit	Text	Kit	Text	Kit
iPaper version of the book	✓	✓	✓	✓	✓	✓
Interactive electronic version of the book	✓					
Fixed tests / progress tests with instant answers	✓		✓			
Mock assessments online			✓	✓		
Material updates	✓	✓	✓	✓	✓	✓
Latest official ACCA exam questions		✓				
Extra question assistance using the signpost icon*		✓				
Timed questions with an online tutor debrief using the clock icon*		✓				
Interim assessment including questions and answers		✓			✓	
Technical articles	✓	✓			✓	✓

* Excludes F1, F2, F3, FFA, FAB, FMA

How to access your online resources

Kaplan Financial students will already have a Kaplan EN-gage account and these extra resources will be available to you online. You do not need to register again, as this process was completed when you enrolled. If you are having problems accessing online materials, please ask your course administrator.

If you are already a registered Kaplan EN-gage user go to www.EN-gage.co.uk and log in. Select the 'add a book' feature and enter the ISBN number of this book and the unique pass key at the bottom of this card. Then click 'finished' or 'add another book'. You may add as many books as you have purchased from this screen.

If you purchased through Kaplan Flexible Learning or via the Kaplan Publishing website you will automatically receive an e-mail invitation to Kaplan EN·gage online. Please register your details using this email to gain access to your content. If you do not receive the e-mail or book content, please contact Kaplan Flexible Learning.

If you are a new Kaplan EN-gage user register at www.EN-gage.co.uk and click on the link contained in the email we sent you to activate your account. Then select the 'add a book' feature, enter the ISBN number of this book and the unique pass key at the bottom of this card. Then click 'finished' or 'add another book'.

Your Code and Information

This code can only be used once for the registration of one book online. This registration and your online content will expire when the final sittings for the examinations covered by this book have taken place. Please allow one hour from the time you submit your book details for us to process your request.

Please scratch the film to access your EN-gage code.

goWB-i4k6-S7KB-7xbu

Please be aware that this code is case-sensitive and you will need to include the dashes within the passcode, but not when entering the ISBN. For further technical support, please visit www.EN-gage.co.uk

Professional Examinations

Level 3

Indirect Tax

FOR ASSESSMENTS FROM 1 JANUARY 2013

REVISION KIT

British Library Cataloguing-in-Publication Data

A catalogue record for this book is available from the British Library.

Published by:

Kaplan Publishing UK

Unit 2 The Business Centre

Molly Millar's Lane

Wokingham

Berkshire

RG41 2QZ

ISBN: 978-0-85732-624-9

© Kaplan Financial Limited, 2013

Printed and bound in Great Britain

Acknowledgements

We are grateful to HM Revenue and Customs for the provision of tax forms, which are Crown Copyright and are reproduced here with kind permission from the Office of Public Sector Information.

CONTENTS

Features in this exam kit

In addition to providing a wide ranging bank of real exam style questions, we have also included in this kit:

- Paper specific information and advice on exam technique.
- Our recommended approach to make your revision for this particular subject as effective as possible.

You will find a wealth of other resources to help you with your studies on the Kaplan and AAT websites:

www.EN-gage.co.uk

www.aat.org.uk

REFERENCE MATERIAL IN YOUR CBT

In the assessment you will be provided with comprehensive Reference Material. You can access this by clicking on the appropriate heading to the right hand side of your computer screen.

The Reference Material is available on the AAT website and is included at the back of the Kaplan ITX combined text/workbook. You should have it available when you work through questions. It is important to know what is in the material and what is not!

Throughout the answers in the kit we have made reference to this material as follows:

Key answer tips

Information about this topic is included in the VAT reference material provided in the real assessment, so you do not need to learn it.

However you need to be familiar with its location and content – why not look at it now?

INDEX TO QUESTIONS AND ANSWERS

PRINCIPLES OF VAT

PREPARING A VAT RETURN AND COMMUNICATING VAT INFORMATION

PAPER ENHANCEMENTS

We have added the following enhancements to the answers in this exam kit:

Key answer tips

Some answers include key answer tips to help your understanding of each question.

Tutorial note

Some answers include more tutorial notes to explain some of the technical points in more detail.

EXAM TECHNIQUE

- **Do not skip any of the material** in the syllabus.

- **Read each question** *very* carefully.

- **Double-check your answer** before committing yourself to it.

- Answer **every** question – if you do not know an answer to a multiple choice question or true/false question, you don't lose anything by guessing. Think carefully before you **guess**.

- If you are answering a multiple-choice question, **eliminate first those answers that you know are wrong**. Then choose the most appropriate answer from those that are left.

- **Don't panic** if you realise you've answered a question incorrectly. Getting one question wrong will not mean the difference between passing and failing

Computer-based exams – tips

- Do not attempt a CBT until you have **completed all study material** relating to it.

- On the AAT website there is a CBT demonstration. It is **ESSENTIAL** that you attempt this before your real CBT. You will become familiar with how to move around the CBT screens and the way that questions are formatted, increasing your confidence and speed in the actual exam.

- Be sure you understand how to use the **software** before you start the exam. If in doubt, ask the assessment centre staff to explain it to you.

- Questions are **displayed on the screen** and answers are entered using keyboard and mouse. At the end of the exam, you are given a certificate showing the result you have achieved.

- In addition to the traditional multiple-choice question type, CBTs will also contain **other types of questions**, such as number entry questions, drag and drop, true/false, pick lists or drop down menus or hybrids of these.

- In some CBTs you will have to type in complete computations or written answers (paper specific).

- You need to be sure you **know how to answer questions** of this type before you sit the exam, through practice.

PAPER SPECIFIC INFORMATION

THE EXAM

FORMAT OF THE ASSESSMENT

The assessment will be divided into **two** sections.

Section 1 covers:

Understanding VAT regulations

- VAT information and registration and HMRC

- VAT documentation, output VAT and input VAT, types of supply

- VAT schemes, record keeping, regulations and penalties

- VAT special cases and correction of errors

- VAT calculations and reconciliation of return to control account

There are five short answer tasks. Some simple calculations will be required. A number of the tasks will be multiple choice or true/false statements.

Section 2 covers:

- VAT return calculations

- Completing the VAT return

- Completion of a piece of written communication

There will be three tasks. These will include the completion of a VAT return from information extracted from the accounting system and a short piece of communication to an internal or external person.

Learners will be required to demonstrate competence in **both** sections of the assessment.

Time allowed

90 minutes

PASS MARK

The pass mark for all AAT CBTs is 70%.

 Always keep your eye on the clock and make sure you attempt all questions!

DETAILED SYLLABUS

The detailed syllabus and study guide written by the AAT can be found at:

www.aat.org.uk

KAPLAN'S RECOMMENDED REVISION APPROACH

QUESTION PRACTICE IS THE KEY TO SUCCESS

Success in professional examinations relies upon you acquiring a firm grasp of the required knowledge at the tuition phase. In order to be able to do the questions, knowledge is essential.

However, the difference between success and failure often hinges on your exam technique on the day and making the most of the revision phase of your studies.

The **Kaplan textbook** is the starting point, designed to provide the underpinning knowledge to tackle all questions. However, in the revision phase, poring over text books is not the answer.

The Kaplan workbook helps you consolidate your knowledge and understanding and is a useful tool to check whether you can remember key topic areas.

Kaplan pocket notes are designed to help you quickly revise a topic area, however you then need to practise questions. There is a need to progress to exam style questions as soon as possible, and to tie your exam technique and technical knowledge together.

The importance of question practice cannot be over-emphasised.

The recommended approach below is designed by expert tutors in the field, in conjunction with their knowledge of the examiner and the specimen assessment.

You need to practise as many questions as possible in the time you have left.

OUR AIM

Our aim is to get you to the stage where you can attempt exam questions confidently, to time, with no supplementary help other than your ITX Reference Material (i.e. to simulate the real examination experience).

Practising your exam technique is also vitally important for you to assess your progress and identify areas of weakness that may need more attention in the final run up to the examination.

Good exam technique is vital.

THE KAPLAN ITX REVISION PLAN

Stage 1: Assess areas of strengths and weaknesses

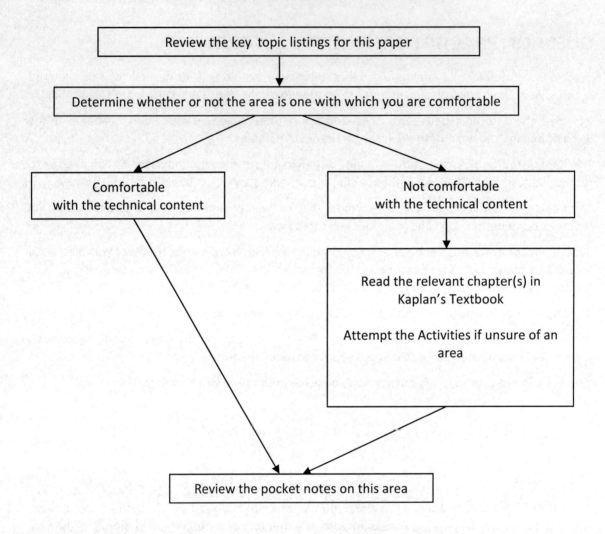

Stage 2: Practise questions

Follow the order of revision of topics as presented in this kit and attempt the questions in the order suggested.

Try to avoid referring to text books and notes and the model answer until you have completed your attempt.

Review your attempt with the model answer and assess how much of the answer you achieved.

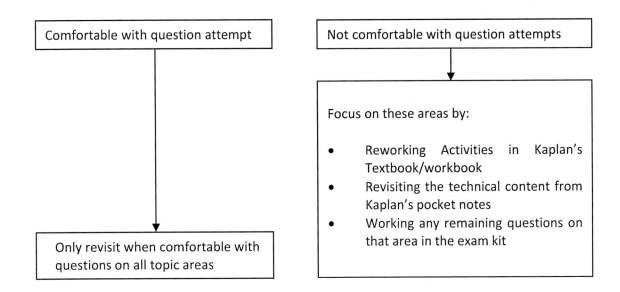

Stage 3: Final pre-exam revision

We recommend that you **attempt at least one mock examination** containing a set of previously unseen exam standard questions.

Attempt the mock CBT online to time with a copy of the AAT reference material to simulate the real exam experience.

You will find a mock CBT for this subject at www.EN-gage.co.uk

REFERENCE INFORMATION

Throughout this exam kit:

1   **You should assume that the reference information given below will continue to apply for the foreseeable future unless you are instructed otherwise.**

2   **Calculations and workings of VAT liability should be made to the nearest penny.**

3   **All apportionments should be made to the nearest month.**

The reference information below contains key numerical information to use in this kit.

Full information is given in the Reference material available on the AAT website and included in the back of the Kaplan combined test/workbook.

Standard rate of VAT	20%
VAT fraction (standard rated)	20/120
(often simplified to 1/6)	
Annual registration limit	£77,000
De – registration limit	£75,000
Cash Accounting:	
Turnover threshold to join scheme	£1,350,000
Turnover threshold to leave scheme	£1,600,000
Annual Accounting:	
Turnover threshold to join scheme	£1,350,000
Turnover threshold to leave scheme	£1,600,000
Flat rate scheme:	
Annual taxable turnover limit (excluding VAT) to join scheme	£150,000
Annual total income (including VAT) to leave scheme	£230,000

Section 1

PRACTICE QUESTIONS

PRINCIPLES OF VAT

REGISTRATION

1   BASSEY

(a)   Bassey asks you which of the following unregistered businesses is **required** to be registered for VAT. All the businesses have been trading for one year.

Select one answer.

A   A business with £77,200 of sales in the last 12 months split evenly between exempt and standard rated supplies

B   A business with £77,200 of sales in the last 12 months split evenly between zero rated and standard rated supplies

C   A business with £77,200 of zero rated sales in the last 12 months

D   A business with £77,200 of exempt sales in the last 12 months

(b)   If you have a query about VAT which of the following actions should you do first?

A   Ring the HMRC helpline

B   Write to HMRC

C   Search the HMRC website

2   WHITMORE

Which two of the following statements are true?

(i)   Whitmore need not register for VAT if he has made £79,000 of taxable supplies in the last 12 months but he expects taxable supplies in the next 12 months to be £76,000.

(ii)   A business has made £80,000 of sales in the last 12 months including £10,000 of sales of capital assets previously used by the business. The business is not required to register at this time.

(iii)   A business which exceeds the registration threshold under the historic test on 31 January will be required to notify HMRC by 2 March and will be registered with effect from 1 March. (Assume it is not a Leap Year).

(iv)   A business which expects to make taxable supplies of £80,000 in the next 30 days must notify HMRC by the end of the 30 day period and will be registered with effect from the end of the 30 day period.

A   (i) and (ii)

B   (ii) and (iii)

C   (iii) and (iv)

D   (i) and (iv)

3   ETO

ETO runs or part runs the following five businesses:

	Taxable supplies per year
Three sole trader businesses	£40,000 each
A business run in partnership with his wife	£100,000
A business run in partnership with his wife and brother	£90,000

How many separate VAT registrations are required to cover these businesses?

A   2

B   3

C   4

D   5

4   JERMAIN

(a)   Jermain is thinking of registering his business for VAT voluntarily rather than waiting until his taxable turnover is over the registration limit.

Which two of the following reasons might explain why a business would not voluntarily register for VAT?

Tick the two correct reasons.

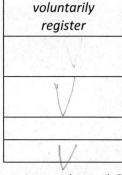

	Would not voluntarily register
It makes their goods more expensive for other VAT registered businesses.	
It makes their goods more expensive for non VAT registered purchasers.	✓
It helps to avoid penalties for late registration.	
It increases the business burden of administration.	✓

(b)   What does Jermain need to demonstrate to HMRC to be able to register voluntarily? Select ONE answer.

A   That he needs to be able to recover his input tax to make his business successful

B   That he intends to make only exempt supplies

C   That he intends to make only zero rated supplies

D   That he intends to make either zero rated or standard rated supplies or both

5   MEERA

(a)   Meera started a business on 1 December. Her monthly sales are £12,000 split equally between standard rated, zero rated and exempt supplies. On what date will she exceed the compulsory VAT registration threshold?

A   Never

B   30 June

C   30 September

D   31 October

(b)   Which TWO of the following will VAT officers normally do during a VAT visit?

A   Examine VAT records

B   Talk to all the staff

C   Watch the business activity

D   Inspect the wages records

E   Complete the latest VAT return

6   VOLUNTARY DEREGISTRATION

Can the following VAT registered traders deregister their business **voluntarily**?

Tick one box on EACH line.

	Yes	No
A business which is ceasing to trade	✗	✓
A continuing business which expects to make supplies of £80,000 in the next year of which one quarter will be exempt supplies	✓	✗
A business which expects to make taxable supplies of £76,000 in the next 12 months		✓
A continuing business which has been making taxable supplies of £80,000 per year but which has now switched to making wholly exempt supplies of the same amount.	✗	✓

7   YODA

Yoda is considering the purchase of one of the following unregistered businesses and wants to know if he should register them for VAT immediately or monitor turnover and register later.

Tick one box on EACH line

	Register now	Monitor and register later
A business with turnover of standard rated supplies of £4,000 per month for the last year but which expects turnover of £50,000 in the next 30 days		✓
A business with £50,000 of taxable turnover in the last 11 months but which expects turnover of £77,000 in the next 30 days	✓	✗
A business with taxable turnover of £5,000 per month for last 12 months		✓
A business with taxable turnover of £6,500 per month for the last 12 months	✓	

8   CERTIFICATE OF REGISTRATION

(a)   Why is a VAT certificate of registration important?

Choose ONE answer.

   A   It is proof that the business has started to trade

   B   It is proof that the business is entitled to charge output VAT

   C   It is proof of the trader's VAT registration number

(b)   Which of the following are powers of HMRC in respect of VAT?

Tick one box on each line.

	Is a power	Is not a power
Charging penalties for breaches of VAT rules	✓	
Completing VAT returns		✓
Inspecting premises	✓	
Providing suitable books for VAT record keeping		✓
Changing the rate of VAT		✓

9   FREDERICK

Which of the following statements is correct?

Select ONE answer.

   A   Frederick should have registered on 1 September. Since that time he has invoiced sales of standard rated goods totalling £10,000. He will be liable for output VAT of £2,000.

   B   The taxable turnover for the historic registration test can be measured at any time, not just the end of the month.

   C   When a trader fails to register on time they can be charged a penalty of up to 100% of the tax due.

   D   All registered traders submit VAT returns quarterly.

10 PICARD

Picard has a business which makes standard rated and zero rated supplies but is not yet registered for VAT. He has given you the following details about his sales.

	Monthly turnover	
	Standard rated	Zero rated
	£	£
Year ended 31 December 20X5	2,000	3,000
January 20X6	2,500	3,100
February 20X6	5,500	4,600
March 20X6	5,800	4,400
April 20X6 and thereafter	6,600	4,900

At the end of which month does Picard exceed the registration limit?

A   February 20X6

B   March 20X6

C   April 20X6

D   December 20X6

VAT DOCUMENTATION

11 NAASIR

(a)   Naasir runs a VAT registered business. On 4 May he receives an order for goods from a customer. On 15 May the goods are delivered and on 20 May Naasir issues a tax invoice. The customer pays on 28 June.

What is the tax point date?

A   4 May

B   15 May

C   20 May

D   28 June

(b)   Daktari is a VAT registered trader. He raises a proforma invoice in advance of making a supply. The proforma invoice is dated 17 August. Payment is received on 20 August and the goods are delivered on 24 August. A VAT invoice is sent to the customer on 31 August.

What is the tax point date?

A   17 August

B   20 August

C   24 August

D   31 August

(c)   Didier is a VAT registered trader. He receives an order for standard rated goods on 1 February, delivers the goods to the customer on 7 February, raises an invoice on 28 February and receives payment on 19 March.

What is the tax point date?

A   1 February

B   7 February

C   28 February

D   19 March

12   AIDAN

(a)   Aidan is a VAT registered trader who makes a mixture of standard rated and zero rated supplies. He makes a wholly zero rated supply to Zed Ltd delivering the goods on 10 July and issuing an invoice on 15 July. He receives payment on 31 July.

Which of the following statements are true?

Tick one box for each line.

	True	False
The tax point date is 10 July.	√	
The tax point date is 15 July.		√
An invoice for a wholly zero rated supply is not a tax invoice.	√	
Input tax recovery in respect of zero rated supplies is restricted		√

(b)   This is a shop invoice for a cash purchase.

South West Supplies,
14, Western Rd,
Cleethorpes
VAT registration number: 123 4567 89
Date: 16 October 20X2

Quantity		£
1	Single bed	389.00
	Total due	389.00
	VAT 20% included	Cash paid

Is this a valid VAT invoice?

Select one of the options below.

A   Yes it is a valid VAT invoice

B   Yes it is a valid simplified VAT invoice

C   Neither of the above

13   **CIARAN**

Ciaran is a registered trader and sells only standard rated goods. His normal terms of trade insist on a 10% deposit as part payment for all sales made. The deposit has to be paid before goods are delivered.

What are the tax points for the deposit and the balance in each of the following?

Complete the table with the appropriate dates.

Deposit paid	Goods delivered	Invoice raised	Balance paid	Tax point for deposit	Tax point for balance
28 June	14 July	17 July	5 August	28–6	17–7
19 October	31 October	16 November	12 December	19–10	31–10
2 December	4 December	22 December	10 December	2–12	4–12

 14 day rule

14   **ELIZABETH**

(a)   Elizabeth is a VAT registered trader. She receives a supplier credit note and processes it in her quarter ended 30 June.

What will be the effect on VAT? Choose one answer.

A   Output tax will increase

B   Output tax will decrease

C   Input tax will increase

D   Input tax will decrease

(b)   A UK business issues a sales invoice for taxable supplies to a VAT registered EU customer.

What is the effect on VAT for the UK business? Choose one answer.

A   Output tax will increase

B   Output tax will stay the same

C   Input tax will decrease

D   Output tax will decrease

15   **ULRIKA**

(a)   Ulrika does not make sales to the public. Which of the following does Ulrika NOT have to include on her sales invoices to other UK businesses?

A   Name and address of the supplier

B   Name and address of the customer

C   VAT registration number of the customer

D   The tax exclusive value of the invoice

(b)   Which of the following does Johnson, a retailer, NOT have to include on his less detailed invoices?

Select one answer.

A   Time of supply

B   Description of each item supplied

C   Rate of VAT applicable to the supply

D   Invoice number

16 AHMED

Ahmed is just starting in business and wants his invoices to comply with VAT rules. He gives you the following list of some of the things he is proposing to include.

Which items are required for a full VAT invoice?

Tick one box for each line.

	Required	Not required
Time of supply	✓	✗
Customer order number		✓
Description of the type of supply	✓	
Rate of VAT applicable	✓	
General terms of trade		✓
Any discount offered	✓	
Total amount payable excluding VAT	✓	
Total amount of VAT payable	✓	
Acceptable methods of payment		✓

17 NERISSA

(a) Nerissa is a VAT registered trader. She has decided to start issuing proforma invoices.

Mark each one of the following statements about proforma invoices as true or false.

	True	False
Proforma invoices are a way of obtaining payment before goods are despatched.	✓	
The purchaser can use a proforma invoice to recover input VAT.		✓
Proforma invoices must show the VAT registration number of the supplier.		✓

(b) Comfy Sofas Ltd normally sell sofas for £600 plus VAT of £120 making a normal selling price of £720. They run a promotion where they offer to pay the customer's VAT. Fred buys a sofa and pays £600.

What is the VAT that Comfy Sofas Ltd must pay over on this sale?

£ 100

18 CHEN

(a) Chen is a VAT registered trader. He issues a sales credit note to a customer.

What will be the effect on VAT? Choose one answer.

A   Input tax will increase

B   Input tax will decrease

C   Output tax will increase

D   Output tax will decrease

(b)   Wing is a VAT registered trader. He receives a supplier credit note.

What effect will this have on the amount of VAT due to HMRC?

Choose one answer.

A   The amount payable will decrease

B   The amount payable will increase

19   EFFIE

(a)   Effie wishes to issue less detailed invoices.

What is the invoice limit above which less detailed invoices cannot be issued?

A   £50

B   £100

C   £200

D   £250

(b)   Effie, who is a retailer, also issues detailed invoices. She asks you which invoice copies she should keep.

Select one option.

A   Less detailed invoices only

B   Detailed invoices only

C   Both

D   Neither

20   HEI

Hei has asked you to advise her which of the following statements about records required for VAT purposes are true and which false.

Tick one box on EACH line.

	True	False
Businesses must keep records of all taxable and exempt supplies made in the course of business.	✓	
Taxpayers need permission from HMRC before they start keeping records electronically.		✓
All businesses must keep a VAT account.	✓	
The balance on the VAT account represents the VAT payable to HMRC or repayable by HMRC.	✓	
Sending or receiving invoices by electronic means is permitted but paper copies must also be kept.		✓
Records should normally be kept for at least 3 years before being destroyed.		✓
Failure to keep records can lead to a penalty.	✓	

21   KYRA

(a)   Kyra makes a taxable supply at a standard rate of 20%. The value of the supply is £900. A trade discount of 10% is applied and a settlement discount of 2% is offered if payment is made within 14 days. The customer does not pay until 30 days after receipt of the invoice.

What is the correct amount of VAT to be shown on the invoice? Choose one answer.

A   £180.00

B   £162.00

C   £158.76

D   £176.40

(b)   Larissa is a VAT registered trader. She sells goods with a VAT exclusive price of £750 to Exe Ltd when the standard rate of VAT is 20%. She does not offer trade discount but she offers a settlement discount of 5% for customers who pay within 7 days and a 2% discount for those paying within 21 days. Exe Ltd pays within 15 days.

What is the correct amount of VAT to be shown on the invoice? Choose one answer.

A   £150.00

B   £142.50

C   £147.00

D   £139.65

(c)   Trina is a VAT registered trader who makes a taxable supply of £240 for which the rate of VAT is 5%. She does not offer a trade discount but offers an 8% settlement discount for payment within 14 days. The customer pays within 14 days

What is the correct amount of VAT to be shown on the invoice? Choose one answer.

A   £48.00

B   £44.16

C   £12.00

D   £11.04

INPUT AND OUTPUT TAX

22   FABRIZIO

Fabrizio's business is VAT registered and supplies goods that are a mix of standard rated and zero rated.

Which of the following statements is true? Choose one answer.

A   None of the input VAT can be reclaimed

B   All of the input VAT can be reclaimed provided certain (de minimis) conditions are met

C   Some of the input VAT can be reclaimed, in proportion to the different types of supply

D   All of the input VAT can be reclaimed

23 ROCCO

Rocco runs a manufacturing business which makes only standard rated supplies. During March the business incurs expenditure of £705 on staff entertaining, £611 on customer entertaining and £8,225 on a second hand van. All figures include VAT at 20%.

What input VAT can be claimed in respect of these three items?

A   £1,590.17

B   £1,488.33

C   £1,472.67

D   £219.33

24 VINCENZO

Vincenzo's business is VAT registered. During June it makes the following cash payments.

Select Yes or No in the right hand box to show whether the input VAT can be reclaimed on the next VAT return.

Description	Net £	VAT £	Gross £	Reclaim input VAT?
Repairs to property	1,900.00	380.00	2,280.00	Yes/No
Delivery van	10,000.00	2,000.00	12,000.00	Yes/No
UK Customer entertaining	640.00	128.00	768.00	Yes/No
Overseas customer entertaining	310.00	62.00	372.00	Yes/No
Car (pool car with no private use)	8,400.00	1,680.00	10,080.00	Yes/No

25 CHO LTD

Cho Ltd is a VAT registered business. The sales manager is provided with a company car and fuel which he uses for both business and private use.

The car has CO$_2$ emissions of 155 gm/km for which the quarterly fuel scale charge is £282. Petrol paid for by the company for the car in the last quarter amounted to £822.50. Both figures are VAT inclusive.

What is the net effect of these on Cho Ltd's VAT for the quarter?

A   VAT payable increases by £80.68

B   VAT payable increases by £90.08

C   VAT payable decreases by £90.08

D   VAT payable decreases by £184.08

26   SOOK

Sook's business is VAT registered and supplies goods that are a mix of standard rated and exempt.

Which of the following statements is true? Choose one answer.

A   None of the input VAT can be reclaimed

B   Input VAT on items used to make exempt supplies can never be recovered

C   Some of the input VAT can be reclaimed, in proportion to the different types of supply

D   All of the input VAT can always be reclaimed

27   JERZY

Jerzy is confused about the difference between making zero rated and exempt supplies. He makes the following statements and wants you to tell him which are true and which false.

Tick one box on EACH line.

	True	False
Traders who make only exempt supplies cannot register for VAT.	✓	
Traders who only make zero rated supplies have to register for VAT.		✓
Zero rated supplies made by a registered trader are not classed as taxable supplies.	~~✓~~	✓
Traders making only exempt supplies cannot recover input tax.	✓	
VAT registered traders making a mix of zero rated and exempt supplies cannot recover any input tax.		✓

28   RAFA AND CO

Rafa and Co wish to avoid paying VAT fuel scale charges in respect of employees' motor expenses.

Which of the following mean they still have to pay a VAT scale charge?

A   The business will only reclaim VAT on fuel used for business mileage and will keep detailed records of business and private mileage driven by employees

B   The business will not reclaim any VAT on fuel

C   The business will only allow employees to claim expenses for fuel for business mileage and will reclaim all input VAT on fuel

D   The business will allow employees to claim 50% of their total fuel costs in their expense claims. The business will then reclaim the input VAT on these 50% costs

29   **FINIAN**

Finian sells a number of capital assets over the year.

Complete the table to show the amount of output VAT that must be charged on the sale of each item.

Item	Input tax recovered	Sale proceeds (excluding VAT)	Output VAT
		£	£.pp
Computer	Yes	400	80
Car	Yes	7,500	1500
Van	Yes	6,100	1220.
Car	No	8,400	0

30   **ALBERT**

Albert is a registered trader who makes only standard rated supplies. In his latest VAT quarter he has spent £780 on a party for all his staff. Each member of staff brought a guest and exactly half the cost of the party was for these guests. Albert also spent £545 on UK customer entertaining and £10,700 on a second hand lorry. All figures include VAT at 20%.

How much input tax can Albert claim on these costs?

A   £2,004.17

B   £1,913.33

C   £1,848.33

D   £2,218.00

31   **VICTORIA LTD**

Victoria Ltd provides a car for an employee who uses the car for both business and private use. All running expenses of the car are paid for by the company including fuel.

Which one of the following statements is true?

A   The company can include all the VAT on running costs in input tax but must then reduce their input tax claim by an amount determined by a scale charge

B   The company cannot recover any VAT on the running costs

C   There is no effect on VAT

D   The company can recover all the VAT on running costs but must add an amount to output tax determined by a scale charge

32 ORSON

Orson is a VAT registered trader who has not adopted any of the special VAT accounting schemes.

Which one of the following statements about recovery of input tax on the purchase of goods is not true?

A   Orson needs to have paid for the goods

B   A VAT invoice is usually needed to support the claim

C   The goods or services must be for business use

D   Input tax cannot be recovered on goods used for customer entertaining

33 MELINDA

Melinda is a VAT registered trader who has suffered input tax on the following purchases over the last quarter.

Can Melinda recover input VAT on these items?

Tick one box on each line.

	Recover	Cannot recover
Purchases for resale	✓	
New laptop computer for Melinda's daughter		✓
New desk for the office (Melinda has lost the VAT receipt)		✓
Motorcycle for business deliveries	✓	

34 NASHEEN

Nasheen is a VAT registered trader who has made the following sales of standard rated items in the previous month.

		£
To AB Ltd (amount inclusive of VAT)	93.6	562
To XY plc (amount exclusive of VAT)	150	750

What is the total output tax on these two supplies? Select one option.

A   £262.40

B   £218.67

C   £237.40

D   £243.67

35 MANINDER

Maninder is a VAT registered trader. During the last quarter she has made the following sales (all figures are exclusive of VAT).

	£	
Standard rated	40,145	8,029
Zero rated	21,050	
Exempt	3,450	
Sale of used plant (Maninder was registered when she purchased this plant)	5,000	1000

How much output VAT should Maninder account for in this quarter? Select ONE option.

A   £7,524.17

B   £9,029.00

C   £13,239.00

D   £8,029.00

36 HARI

Hari wishes to claim bad debt relief on a sales invoice to Zed Ltd with VAT of £145.

Which of the following are not requirements for Hari to be able to claim VAT bad debt relief?

Select two answers.

A   The debt must have been written off in the accounting records for at least three months before the claim is made

B   Hari has already paid over the output tax of £145 to HMRC

C   Zed Ltd has been placed into liquidation

D   Six months have passed since the invoice was due for payment

ACCOUNTING SCHEMES

37 EXE LTD

(a)   Exe Ltd has not joined any of the special accounting schemes. Its quarterly return period ends on 31 July.

By what date should their VAT return be submitted?

Select one answer.

A   31 August

B   6 September

C   7 September

D   None of the above

(b)   If Exe Ltd submits their VAT return late for the first time, what is the effect?

Select one answer.

A   A surcharge of 5% of VAT due is charged

B   A surcharge liability notice is issued

C   Both of the above

D   Neither of the above

38   RAVI

Ravi has asked you to advise him whether the following statements about businesses that have not joined any special schemes are true or false.

Tick one box for EACH line

	True	False
VAT is normally payable at the same time that the return is due	✓	
Paying VAT by direct debit gives the business an extra 5 bank working days from the normal payment date before payment is taken from the account.		✓
New businesses have a choice about whether they submit returns electronically or on paper.		✓
Quarterly VAT returns are all made up to 30 April, 31 July, 31 October and 31 January		✓

39   ANNUAL ACCOUNTING

(a)   What is the turnover limit for eligibility to join the annual accounting scheme? Select ONE answer.

   A   Estimated turnover in the next 12 months is not more than £150,000

   B   Estimated turnover in the next 12 months is not more than £230,000

   C   Estimated turnover in the next 12 months is not more than £1,350,000

   D   Estimated turnover in the next 12 months is not more than £1,600,000

(b)   With the annual accounting scheme, one VAT return is made each year.

   How many months after the end of the accounting period end is the return due? Choose one answer.

   A   1 month

   B   2 months

   C   3 months

   D   4 months

(c)   Wye Ltd is a company that sells children's clothing. This is a zero rated activity.

   Is Wye Ltd likely to benefit from joining the annual accounting scheme?

   A   Yes

   B   No

(d)   Queue Ltd is a VAT registered business whose turnover of taxable supplies has been declining for several years.

   Is Queue likely to benefit from joining the annual accounting scheme?

   A   Yes

   B   No

40   ZED LTD

Zed Ltd is a company that uses the annual accounting scheme for VAT with monthly (not quarterly) payments. Their VAT liability for the previous accounting period was £72,900.

What is their monthly payment on account for the current year?

A   12 monthly payments of £6,075

B   12 monthly payments of £5,468

C   9 monthly payments of £7,290

D   9 monthly payments of £8,100

41   TARAN

Taran runs a VAT registered business and needs more information about the annual accounting scheme.

Which of the following statements are true and which false?

Tick one box for EACH line.

	True	False
Taxpayers must be up to date with their VAT returns before they are allowed to join the scheme.	√	
Monthly payments on account are 10% of the previous year's VAT liability.	√	
Monthly payments can be made using any method convenient to the taxpayer.		√
Monthly payments are made 7 days after the end of months 2 to 10 in the accounting period.		√
The scheme allows businesses to budget for their VAT payments more easily.	√	

42   ARTHUR

Which of the following statements on the subject of cash accounting are true?

Select TWO answers.

A   Input VAT is reclaimed by reference to the date the supplier is paid

B   Traders can join the scheme provided their annual taxable turnover does not exceed £1,600,000

C   VAT invoices do not need to be sent to customers

D   Arthur is a VAT registered trader whose annual turnover excluding VAT is £400,000. He has never had any convictions for VAT offences. He is eligible to join the cash accounting scheme.

43 LAREDO

Laredo is a VAT registered trader who has adopted the cash accounting scheme. He receives an order from a customer on 13 March and despatches the goods on 20 March. He invoices the customer on 24 March and receives payment on 2 May.

What is the tax point date?

A   13 March

B   20 March

C   24 March

D   2 May

44 CASH ACCOUNTING

Would the following VAT registered businesses benefit from joining the cash accounting scheme?

Tick one box on EACH line

	Will benefit	Will not benefit
A manufacturing business that sells all its output on credit to other businesses. Debtors take on average 45 days to pay. The business aims to pay creditors within 30 days of receiving purchase invoices.	✓	
A clothes shop based in a town centre which sells standard rated supplies to members of the public for cash.		✓
A wholesaler who sells to other businesses on 40 days credit. In the last 12 months the business has suffered a steep rise in bad debts.	✓	
A business making solely zero rated supplies to other businesses.		✓

45 FLAT RATE SCHEME

Would the following VAT registered businesses benefit from joining the flat rate scheme?

	Will benefit	Will not benefit
A business making solely zero rated supplies to other businesses.		✓
A business with a lower than average (for their trade sector) level of input tax.	✓	
A business with a higher level of standard rated supplies than other businesses in the same trade sector.	✓	

46   RAY

Ray makes the following statements about the flat rate scheme.

Which of the statements are true and which false?

Tick one box on EACH line.

	True	False
A business can join the flat rate scheme provided their taxable turnover for the next 12 months is expected to be less than £230,000.		✓
VAT due to HMRC is calculated as a fixed percentage of VAT inclusive taxable turnover.		✓
VAT invoices must still be issued.	✓	
A business can be in both the flat rate scheme and the annual accounting scheme at the same time.	✓	
The scheme cuts down on the time spent on VAT administration.	✓	
Businesses cannot pay less VAT under the flat rate scheme than the normal method of accounting for VAT.		✓

47   FENFANG

In the last quarter, Fenfang has made sales as follows:

	£
Standard rated sales (including VAT)	22,470
Zero rated sales	4,500
Exempt sales	1,110

The flat rate percentage for her business is 8%.

What is her VAT payable for the quarter?

A   £1,797.60

B   £2,157.60

C   £2,246.40

D   £1,498.00

ERRORS AND PENALTIES

48 VAT PENALTIES

Which of the statements are true and which false?

Tick one box on EACH line.

	True	False
Tax avoidance is a criminal offence and means using illegal means to reduce tax liability.	✓	✓
A penalty can be charged if a trader fails to register at the correct time.	✓	
A registered trader who makes an error on a return leading to underpayment of tax will always be charged a penalty.		✓
If a registered trader does not submit a VAT return then HMRC can issue an assessment to collect VAT due.	✓	

49 VAT ERRORS

(a) For each of the following businesses, indicate with a tick whether the non deliberate error can be corrected on the next VAT return or whether separate disclosure is required.

	Net error £	Turnover £	Include in next return	Separate disclosure
1	24,567	2,000,000		✓
2	4,568	85,400	✓	
3	35,980	4,567,090	✓	
4	51,600	10,000,000		✓

(b) A business discovers the following non deliberate errors made in the previous quarter.

(i) VAT on a sales credit note has been recorded as £18 instead of £81

(ii) VAT of £21.14 on a supplier invoice has been entered twice.

What is the net error?

£ 41.86

Will the error increase or reduce the VAT due on the next return

Increase/reduce

Sales credit note

Vat output 81 - 18 = 63

Vat input - 21.14.

- 63
+21.14
41.86

50   DEFAULT SURCHARGE

(a)   Which of the following statements about the default surcharge are correct?

Tick one box on each line.

	True	False
A default only occurs when a business pays its VAT late.		✓
A surcharge liability notice lasts for 6 months from the end of the period of default.	✗	✓
Once a trader has received a surcharge liability notice, he must keep all his returns and payments up to date for the period of the surcharge notice, otherwise it will be extended.	✓	

(b)   At 31.3.X0, the VAT control account of Z Ltd showed a balance due to HMRC of £4,937.50. The VAT return for the quarter showed VAT due of £2,452.10.

Which of the following explains the difference? Choose one answer.

A   A VAT payment to HMRC of £2,485.40 has been included twice in the VAT control account

B   Output VAT of £2,485.40 has been included twice in the VAT control account.

PREPARING A VAT RETURN AND COMMUNICATING VAT INFORMATION

VAT RETURNS AND COMMUNICATIONS

51 PATEL

Patel is a registered trader. He has written off the following debts on 30.9.X1:

Amount	Date of supply	Date payment due
£4,200	15.1.X1	28.1.X1
£6,552	6.3.X1	30.3.X1
£7,000	10.4.X1	30.3.X1
£2,500	7.5.X1	31.5.X1

All amounts are inclusive of 20% VAT.

What is the total VAT bad debt relief that can be claimed in the quarter ended 30.9.X1?

2,958.6

52 DAVIES LTD

The following accounts have been extracted from a company's ledgers:

Date		Dr	Cr
		£	£
Purchases:UK			
31.3.X2	Purchases day book	69,200	
30.4.X2	Purchases day book	63,180	
31.5 X2	Purchases day book	67,340	
Sales: UK			
31.3.X2	Sales day book		121,000
30.4.X2	Sales day book		179,020
31.5 X2	Sales day book		140,800
Sales: Export EU			
31.3.X2	Sales day book		30,300
30.4.X2	Sales day book		41,160
31.5 X2	Sales day book		35,780
Sales: Exports non EU			
31.3.X2	Sales day book		17,000
30.4.X2	Sales day book		14,900
31.5 X2	Sales day book		20,200
VAT: Output Tax			
31.3.X2	Sales day book		24,200
30.4.X2	Sales day book		35,804
31.5 X2	Sales day book		28,160
VAT: Input tax			
31.3.X2	Purchases day book	13,840	
30.4.X2	Purchases day book	12,636	
31.5 X2	Purchases day book	13,468	

199720·

440820·

107240

52100

88164

39944

You are given the following further information.

(1)   VAT returns are completed quarterly and submitted electronically.

(2)   All EU exports are to VAT registered customers

(3)   Payments are made by electronic bank transfer.

(4)   An error was made in the previous return. Input tax was over claimed by £5,450.95.

(5)   Today's date is 19 June 20X2.

Complete Boxes 1 to 9 of the following VAT return for the quarter ended 31 May 20X2.

		£
VAT due in this period on **sales** and other outputs	**Box 1**	88164
VAT due in this period on **acquisitions** from other **EC Member States**	**Box 2**	0
Total VAT due (**the sum of boxes 1 and 2**)	**Box 3**	88164
VAT reclaimed in the period on **purchases** and other inputs, including acquisitions from the EC	**Box 4**	34,493.05
Net VAT to be paid to HM Revenue & Customs or reclaimed by you (**Difference between boxes 3 and 4**)	**Box 5**	53670.95
Total value of **sales** and all other outputs excluding any VAT. **Include your box 8 figure**	**Box 6**	600160
Total value of purchases and all other inputs excluding any VAT. **Include your box 9 figure**	**Box 7**	199720
Total value of all **supplies** of goods and related costs, excluding any VAT, to other **EC Member States**	**Box 8**	107.240
Total value of all **acquisitions** of goods and related costs, excluding any VAT, from other **EC Member States**	**Box 9**	0

39.944.
−5450.95

53 DHONI LTD

You are an accounting technician who has prepared the VAT return for Dhoni Ltd for the quarter ended 31 December 20X2.

Today's date is 17 January 20X3.

In the previous quarter output VAT was understated by £4,672.90. In the current quarter the figure from Box 6 of the return is £210,050.

Complete the following email to the financial accountant explaining whether the error can be corrected on the VAT return to 31 December 20X2.

For words in bold, select the correct word/phrase.

Email

To: *Financial account*

From: *Accounting technician*

Date: *17 Jan 20X3*

Subject: *error understated / VAT error*

An error occurred in the VAT return for the previous quarter. Output VAT of £4,672.90 was (over/**understated**). This resulted in VAT being (over/**under paid**).

This error (**was included on the VAT return to 31 December** /must be separately notified to HMRC).

Kind regards

---

54 JASPER

Jasper runs a UK business selling standard rated golf accessories. He imports some items from overseas, both from other EU countries and from outside the EU. All purchases are items that would be standard rated in the UK.

The VAT rate is 20%.

In the quarter ended 30 June 20X2 his purchases are as follows:

	£
Purchases from UK businesses	54,800
Purchases from EU registered businesses	27,400
Purchases from outside the EU	37,600

All these figures exclude VAT.

Complete Boxes 2, 4, 7 and 9 of the VAT return below.

		£
VAT due in this period on **sales** and other outputs	Box 1	
VAT due in this period on **acquisitions** from other **EC Member States**	Box 2	5480
Total VAT due (**the sum of boxes 1 and 2**)	Box 3	
VAT reclaimed in the period on **purchases** and other inputs, including acquisitions from the EC	Box 4	23960
Net VAT to be paid to HM Revenue & Customs or reclaimed by you (**Difference between boxes 3 and 4**)	Box 5	
Total value of **sales** and all other outputs excluding any VAT. **Include your box 8 figure**	Box 6	
Total value of purchases and all other inputs excluding any VAT. **Include your box 9 figure**	Box 7	119 800
Total value of all **supplies** of goods and related costs, excluding any VAT, to other **EC Member States**	Box 8	
Total value of all **acquisitions** of goods and related costs, excluding any VAT, from other **EC Member States**	Box 9	27 400

55 TROTT

From the summarised daybooks below, complete the VAT return for the quarter to 31 March 20X5.

Trott does not use any special VAT accounting scheme.

Sales day book

		Total £	VAT £	UK Sales £
Total	31 March 20X5	8,820.00	1,470.00	7,350.00

Sales credit notes day book

		Total £	VAT £	UK Sales £
Total	31 March 20X5	420.00	70.00	350.00

Purchase day book

		Total £	VAT £	Purchases £	Other Expenses £
Total	31 March 20X5	4,332.00	722.00	2,160.00	1,450.00

Cash receipts book

		Total £	VAT £	Cash Sales £	Cash from Debtors £
Total	31 March 20X5	5,092.00	52.00	260.00	4,780.00

Cash payments book

		Total £	VAT £	Cash Purchases £	Pay to Creditors £
Total	31 March 20X5	4,230.00	30.00	150.00	4,050.00

Petty cash book

		Total £	VAT £	Sundry £
Total	31 March 20X5	198.00	33.00	165.00

Trott gives you the following additional information.

39 vat

Trott has written off as a bad debt an amount of £235 (including VAT) which was due for payment 8 months before.

1470 -70
+52

722 +30
+33 +39

		£
VAT due in this period on **sales** and other outputs	Box 1	1452.
VAT due in this period on **acquisitions** from other **EC Member States**	Box 2	0
Total VAT due (**the sum of boxes 1 and 2**)	Box 3	1452.
VAT reclaimed in the period on **purchases** and other inputs, including acquisitions from the EC	Box 4	824.16
Net VAT to be paid to HM Revenue & Customs or reclaimed by you (**Difference between boxes 3 and 4**)	Box 5	627.84.
Total value of **sales** and all other outputs excluding any VAT. **Include your box 8 figure**	Box 6	7260
Total value of purchases and all other inputs excluding any VAT. **Include your box 9 figure**	Box 7	3925
Total value of all **supplies** of goods and related costs, excluding any VAT, to other **EC Member States**	Box 8	0
Total value of all **acquisitions** of goods and related costs, excluding any VAT, from other **EC Member States**	Box 9	0.

56 BELL

You are an accounting technician working for a firm of accountants. You have just completed the VAT return for the quarter to 31 March 20X5 for one of your clients, Andrew Bell.

Andrew Bell wrote off a debt of £6,467 on 28 February 20X5. This debt had been outstanding since 15 August 20X4.

Complete the following email to Bell explaining how you have dealt with the bad debt.

For words in bold, select the correct word/phrase. The date is 17 April 20X5.

Email

To: *Andrew Bell*

From: *Accounting technician*

Date: *17 – April X5*

Subject: *VAT Return*

Thank you for advising me about the debt you wrote off. I have included relief for this in the VAT return for the quarter ended (.........*31 March 20X0*.........).

Relief can be claimed because the debt was due for payment more than (**3 months/6 months**) ago.

The (**input/output**) tax paid on the original invoice can be reclaimed by including the amount in (**Box1/Box4**). The amount of bad debt relief is (£...*10.77.83*...).

Kind regards

57 MISTRY

This task is about preparing figures for a VAT return for the period ended 31 March 20X0.

The standard rate of VAT is 20%.

The business's EU acquisitions are goods that would normally be standard rated.

The following accounts have been extracted from the business's ledgers:

Sales and sales returns account					
Date 20X0	Reference	Debit £	Date 20X0	Reference	Credit £
01/01 – 31/03	Sales returns daybook – UK sales returns	9,000.00	01/01 – 31/03	Sales daybook – UK sales	670,000.00
31/03	Balance c/d	759,200.00	01/01 – 31/03	Sales daybook – EU dispatches	98,200.00
	Total	768,200.00		Total	768,200.00

Purchases account					
Date 20X0	Reference	Debit £	Date 20X0	Reference	Credit £
01/01 – 31/03	Purchases day book – UK purchases	311,000.00	31/03	Balance c/d	360,000.00
01/01 – 31/03	Purchases daybook – EU acquisitions	15,000.00			
01/01 – 31/03	Purchases daybook – zero rated imports	34,000.00			
	Total	360,000.00		Total	360,000.00

VAT account (Incomplete)					
Date 20X0	Reference	Debit £	Date 20X0	Reference	Credit £
01/01 – 31/03	Sales returns daybook	1,800.00	01/01 – 31/03	Sales daybook	134,000.00
01/01 – 31/03	Purchases daybook	62,200.00			

EU dispatches and acquisitions are with VAT registered businesses.

(a)   Calculate the figure for Box 2 of the VAT return – VAT due on acquisitions from other EC member states

2000

(b)   Calculate the figure for Box 1 of the VAT return – VAT due on sales and other outputs

132 200

(c)   Calculate the figure for Box 4 of the VAT return – VAT reclaimed on purchases and other inputs, including acquisitions from the EC

64200   62.200 + 2000

58   BARTLET LTD

Complete the VAT return given using the information below which is taken from the summarised daybooks and petty cash book for the quarter ended 30 September 20X2

	Net £.pp	VAT £.pp	Total £.pp
Sales day book			
UK Standard rated sales	20,500.00	4,100.00	24,600.00
UK zero rated sales	13,470.00	Nil	13,470.00
UK exempt sales	1,650.00	N/A	1,650.00
Sales to VAT registered EU customers	5,105.00	Nil	5,105.00
Sales to non VAT registered EU customers	1,200.00	240.00	1,440.00
Exports outside the EU	3,750.00	Nil	3,750.00
	45 675		
Purchases day book			
UK purchases and expenses	17,000.00	3,400.00	20,400.00
Purchases from EU businesses	2,860.00	572.00	3,432.00
Petty cash book			
UK purchases and expenses	640.00	128.00	768.00
	20 500		

(i)   The business has no cash sales or purchases recorded in the cash books.

(ii)   No partial exemption adjustment is required.

(iii)   The business files returns quarterly and uses electronic filing and payment.

(iv)   As well as the purchases above, the business has incurred wages costs of £5,600 in the quarter.

(v)   The date is 20 October 20X2.

		£
VAT due in this period on **sales** and other outputs	**Box 1**	4340
VAT due in this period on **acquisitions** from other **EC Member States**	**Box 2**	572
Total VAT due (**the sum of boxes 1 and 2**)	**Box 3**	4912.
VAT reclaimed in the period on **purchases** and other inputs, including acquisitions from the EC	**Box 4**	4100
Net VAT to be paid to HM Revenue & Customs or reclaimed by you (**Difference between boxes 3 and 4**)	**Box 5**	812.
Total value of **sales** and all other outputs excluding any VAT. **Include your box 8 figure**	**Box 6**	45678
Total value of purchases and all other inputs excluding any VAT. **Include your box 9 figure**	**Box 7**	20 500
Total value of all **supplies** of goods and related costs, excluding any VAT, to other **EC Member States**	**Box 8**	5105
Total value of all **acquisitions** of goods and related costs, excluding any VAT, from other **EC Member States**	**Box 9**	2860

59   SEABORN LTD

Seaborn Ltd is a new company that has just registered for VAT. It makes mainly standard rated supplies with a few zero rated supplies. It does not use any special accounting schemes.

You are an accounting technician. Today's date is 5 September 20X6.

Complete the following email to the financial accountant advising generally when VAT returns must be filed. For words in bold, select the correct word/phrase.

Email

To: *Financial accountant*

From: *Accounting technician*

Date: *5 September 20X6.*

Subject: *VAT return*

VAT returns must be submitted (**monthly/quarterly/yearly**) unless you are a net repayment trader when returns can be made (**monthly/quarterly/yearly**).

Returns must be filed within (**30 days/1 month/3 months**) after the end of the VAT period with an extension of (**3 days/7 days/2 weeks**) where returns are filed online.

You (**have a choice as to whether you file returns on paper or online/must file online**).

Kind regards

---

60   KEIKO LTD

Keiko Ltd is a business that uses cash accounting scheme. All sales and purchases are standard rated.

You are given the following information for the quarter ended 31 May 20X5:

	£
Sales invoices issued for credit sales	42,568
Purchase invoices received from suppliers	29,580
Cash sales receipts	780
Receipts from debtors	39,745
Cash paid to creditors	27,890
Petty cash – purchases of standard rated items	175

Calculate how much VAT Keiko Ltd owes for the quarter to 31 May 20X5.

61   O'BRIEN

You are given the following summaries of the sales and purchases daybooks and the cash book of O'Brien.

Use the information to complete the VAT return for the quarter ended 30 June 20X2.

	April £	May £	June £	Total £
SALES DAY BOOK SUMMARY				
UK standard rated sales	11,775.00	9,861.56	8,235.50	29,872.06
UK zero rated sales	34,567.00	33,694.50	29,385.64	97,647.14
Sales to EU registered businesses	5,000.00	3,600.00	8,650.00	17,250.00
VAT	2,355.00	1,972.31	1,647.10	5,974.41
	53,697.00	49,128.37	47,918.24	150,743.61
PURCHASE DAY BOOK SUMMARY				
Purchases	28,350.00	21,670.65	20,924.50	70,945.15
Expenses	4,780.00	2,559.50	8,891.67	16,231.17
VAT	6,626.00	4,846.03	5,963.23	17,435.26
	39,756.00	29,076.18	35,779.40	104,611.58
CASH PAYMENTS BOOK SUMMARY				
To creditors	39,457.10	35,682.50	27,420.56	102,560.16
For wages	5,010.00	5,196.50	5,259.96	15,466.46
Cash purchases	250.00	367.50	482.00	1,099.50
VAT	50.00	73.50	96.40	219.90
	44,767.10	41,320.00	33,258.92	119,346.02
CASH RECEIPTS BOOK SUMMARY				
From debtors	49,845.66	51,793.78	49,382.55	151,021.99
Cash sales (all UK)	1,000.00	750.00	2,150.50	3,900.50
VAT	200.00	150.00	430.10	780.10
	51,045.66	52,693.78	51,963.15	155,702.59

In addition to providing the summaries above, O'Brien tells you the following:

(i)   He made a non deliberate and non careless error in the output tax included on his last return. This was understated by £8,100.

(ii)   O'Brien has a car which he uses for both business and private purposes. All the costs are charged through the business including fuel for private use. The VAT fuel scale charge for a quarter for the car is £326 (VAT inclusive).

		£
VAT due in this period on **sales** and other outputs	Box 1	*14908.84*
VAT due in this period on **acquisitions** from other **EC Member States**	Box 2	*0*
Total VAT due (**the sum of boxes 1 and 2**)	Box 3	*14908.84*
VAT reclaimed in the period on **purchases** and other inputs, including acquisitions from the EC	Box 4	*17655.16*
Net VAT to be paid to HM Revenue & Customs or reclaimed by you (**Difference between boxes 3 and 4**)	Box 5	*−2746.32*
Total value of **sales** and all other outputs excluding any VAT. **Include your box 8 figure**	Box 6	*148669.*
Total value of purchases and all other inputs excluding any VAT. **Include your box 9 figure**	Box 7	*88275.*
Total value of all **supplies** of goods and related costs, excluding any VAT, to other **EC Member States**	Box 8	*17 250.*
Total value of all **acquisitions** of goods and related costs, excluding any VAT, from other **EC Member States**	Box 9	*0.*

Handwritten margin notes (left): 5974.41 / 780.10 / 8100 / 84.33 / 17.435.26 / 219.40

Handwritten notes (right of Box 6): +2716 / 149406

62   MILES

Miles is a registered trader who uses his car for both business and personal use. His personal use is approximately 20%. He keeps detailed records of all his business and private mileage. He is anxious to know if he can reclaim input VAT on the running costs of his car.

You are an Accounting technician. Miles has consulted you about his motoring costs.

Complete the following email to O'Brien For words in bold, select the correct word/phrase.

Today's date is 14 July 20X2

Email

To: *Miles*

From: *Accounting technical*

Date: *14 July X2*

Subject: VAT and cars

Input VAT on the purchase of a car for both business and private use **(can/~~cannot~~)** be recovered.

Generally input VAT on all car running costs can be recovered but only if you account for a VAT scale charge.

The VAT exclusive element of this scale charge is **(added to inputs in Box 7/ added to outputs in Box 6).**

The VAT element of the scale charge is **(added to input tax in Box 4/ added to output tax in Box 1).**

If you do not wish to account for a VAT fuel charge you can **(reclaim only 20% of your input VAT/reclaim only 80% of your input VAT).**

Kind regards

---

63   SPRINGER

Springer is a sole trader whose business is registered for VAT. He does not use any special accounting schemes. All his sales and purchases are standard rated for VAT.

He gives you the following information about transactions for the quarter ended 31 December 20X3:

	£
Sales invoices issued for credit sales	67,800
Purchase invoices received from suppliers	45,350
Cash sales receipts	235
Sales credit notes issued	1,980
Purchase debit notes issued	2,100
Petty cash – purchases of standard rated items	155

What is the amount of VAT due from Springer for the quarter ended 31 December 20X3?

64 STEWART LTD (1)

The following accounts have been extracted from a company's ledgers at the end of the quarter to 31 October 20X5:

	Dr £	Cr £
Purchases – UK	59,678	
Purchases – EU businesses	14,593	
Purchase credit notes – UK		2,569
Expenses (all standard rated)	19,437	
Wages and salaries	8,750	
Sales – UK		145,450
Sales credit notes	3,568	
VAT – input tax on UK purchases and expenses	15,309.20	
VAT – output tax on UK sales		28,376.61

(i) The financial accountant is aware that the company needs to do something about VAT on the purchases from EU businesses but no entries have been made in the ledger for the VAT on these yet. *2918.60*

(ii) Stewart Ltd also has received the following invoice, which relates to the quarter ended 31 October 20X5, but which has not yet been included in the records.

	Gross £	VAT £	Net £
Purchase of a lorry	24,000.00	4,000.00	20,000.00

(iii) The company files its VAT returns and pays its VAT electronically.

Prepare a VAT return for the quarter ended 31 October 20X5.

		£
VAT due in this period on **sales** and other outputs	Box 1	28376.61
VAT due in this period on **acquisitions** from other **EC Member States**	Box 2	2918.60
Total VAT due (**the sum of boxes 1 and 2**)	Box 3	31295.21
VAT reclaimed in the period on **purchases** and other inputs, including acquisitions from the EC	Box 4	22.227 8
Net VAT to be paid to HM Revenue & Customs or reclaimed by you (**Difference between boxes 3 and 4**)	Box 5	9067.41
Total value of **sales** and all other outputs excluding any VAT. **Include your box 8 figure**	Box 6	141812
Total value of purchases and all other inputs excluding any VAT. **Include your box 9 figure**	Box 7	191139
Total value of all **supplies** of goods and related costs, excluding any VAT, to other **EC Member States**	Box 8	0
Total value of all **acquisitions** of goods and related costs, excluding any VAT, from other **EC Member States**	Box 9	14593

65 STEWART LTD (2)

Refer to the information in Stewart Ltd (1) above.

Complete the following email to the financial accountant about the capital expenditure in the period and the date the return will be due.

For words in bold, select the correct word/phrase. Today's date is 17 November 20X5

Email

To: Financial accountant

From: Accountant tech

Date: 17 - Nov - X5

Subject: Capital expenditure

Please be advised that I have just completed the VAT return for the quarter ended (..31..Oct..2X5..). The amount of VAT **(payable/receivable)** will be (£...9,067..41......).

The return must be with HMRC on or before (....7 Dec.....).

The VAT will be **(paid electronically by ......7 Dec....../received directly into our bank account)**.

I have included the invoice for capital expenditure. VAT of (£.....4000....) can be reclaimed on this expenditure.

Kind regards

Section 2

ANSWERS TO PRACTICE QUESTIONS

PRINCIPLES OF VAT

REGISTRATION

1   BASSEY

(a)   The answer is B.

The historic registration test is based on a business achieving £77,000 of taxable turnover in the last 12 months or since starting in business if this is less than 12 months. Taxable turnover excludes exempt supplies and for registration purposes it also excludes the sale of capital assets.

In A the business has only £38,600 of taxable turnover and in D it has none.

A business that only makes zero rated sales can choose to claim exemption from registration when it has more than £77,000 of taxable turnover. C is therefore not **required** to **be** registered.

(b)   The answer is C

Key answer tips

Information about this topic is included in the VAT reference material provided in the real assessment, so you do not need to learn it.

However you need to be familiar with its location and content – why not look at it now?

2   WHITMORE

The answer is B.

Statement (i) is false as Whitmore would have to be expecting taxable supplies of less than the deregistration limit of £75,000 in the next 12 months to avoid having to register now.

Statement (ii) is true. Sales of capital assets are not included in the total of taxable supplies for registration purposes. Hence the business has made only £70,000 of relevant taxable supplies and as this is less than the registration limit of £77,000, the business does not need to register.

Statement (iii) is true. Businesses must notify HMRC within 30 days of the end of the month in which the registration limit is exceeded and will be registered from the start of the month which starts one month after exceeding the limit.

Statement (iv) is largely correct but the business will be registered with effect from the **start** of the 30 day period, not the end.

Key answer tips

Make sure you read written questions like this thoroughly.

Part (iv) looks correct at first reading. You have to look at it carefully to notice the error.

3   ETO

The answer is B.

Sole traders have one registration covering their businesses but not those they run in partnership with others.

The two partnerships must be separately registered.

This makes 3 registrations in total.

Tutorial note

A sole trader has a single registration covering all the businesses they run as a sole trader. So it is the combined turnover of all their businesses that must be checked to see if it is over the registration limit. In this case Eto has £120,000 from his sole trader businesses and must register.

*Separate partnerships, but with the same partners, must also have a single registration, so if Eto and **only** his wife ran another business in partnership they would have to include that in their partnership registration.*

Companies are individually registered.

4   JERMAIN

(a)   Voluntary registration

	Would not voluntarily register
It makes their goods more expensive for other VAT registered businesses.	
It makes their goods more expensive for non VAT registered purchasers.	√
It helps to avoid penalties for late registration.	
It increases the business burden of administration.	√

(b)   The answer is D.

Tutorial note

Voluntary registration is open to all businesses that make, or intend to make, taxable supplies.

Voluntary registration is useful because:

1   It avoids the possibility of penalties for late registration.

2   It disguises the small size of the business.

3   It is useful for business' that sell zero rated goods to register as they can still reclaim the Input VAT (VAT on purchases).

Disadvantages of voluntary registration include:

1   It increases the burden of administration for small businesses.

2   It causes the sales price of goods to be increased by the addition of VAT. This is only a problem for those, like the public, who cannot recover VAT. Other VAT registered businesses can recover the VAT so this would not be a reason for not voluntarily registering.

5   MEERA

(a)   The answer is C.

Taxable turnover is £8,000 per month and after ten months, at the end of September; the business will have made £80,000 of taxable supplies.

Tutorial note

The historic registration test is based on a business achieving £77,000 of taxable turnover in the last 12 months or since starting in business if this is less than 12 months. Taxable turnover excludes exempt supplies but includes zero rated supplies.

(b)   The answers are A and C.

Key answer tips

Information about this topic is included in the VAT reference material provided in the real assessment, so you do not need to learn it.

However you need to be familiar with its location and content – why not look at it now?

6 VOLUNTARY DEREGISTRATION

	Yes	No
A business which is ceasing to trade		√
A continuing business which expects to make supplies of £80,000 in the next year of which one quarter will be exempt supplies	√	
A business which expects to make taxable supplies of £72,000 in the next 12 months		√
A continuing business which has been making taxable supplies of £80,000 per year but which has now switched to making wholly exempt supplies of the same amount.		√

Tutorial note

A business can deregister if its expected taxable turnover for the next 12 months is below the deregistration limit (currently £75,000).

A business which has ceased to trade or which switches to making wholly exempt supplies MUST deregister. They cannot deregister voluntarily.

In the example above, only the second business can deregister voluntarily. They are expecting to make taxable supplies in the next 12 months of £60,000 which is below the deregistration limit.

Key answer tips

Information about this topic is included in the VAT reference material provided in the real assessment, so you do not need to learn it.

However you need to be familiar with its location and content – why not look at it now?

7 YODA

	Register now	Monitor and register later
A business with turnover of standard rated supplies of £4,000 per month for the last year but which expects turnover of £50,000 in the next 30 days		√
A business with £50,000 of taxable turnover in the last 11 months but which expects turnover of £77,000 in the next 30 days	√	
A business with taxable turnover of £5,000 per month for last 12 months		√
A business with taxable turnover of £6,500 per month for the last 12 months	√	

Tutorial note

The historic registration test is based on achieving £77,000 of taxable turnover in the last 12 months or since starting in business if this is less than 12 months.

The future turnover test says that a business must register if taxable turnover of more than the registration limit is expected in the next 30 days.

The second business has to register under the future test as they are expecting £77,000 of turnover in the next 30 days and the fourth business under the historic test (12 months × £6,500 = £78,000).

Key answer tips

Information about this topic is included in the VAT reference material provided in the real assessment, so you do not need to learn it.

However you need to be familiar with its location and content – why not look at it now?

8 CERTIFICATE OF REGISTRATION

(a) The answer is C

(b) HMRC powers

	Is a power	Is not a power
Charging penalties for breaches of VAT rules	√	
Completing VAT returns		√
Inspecting premises	√	
Providing suitable books for VAT record keeping		√
Changing the rate of VAT		√

Tutorial note

The certificate of registration proves that a business is registered for VAT. It shows the VAT registration number which must be shown on their invoices.

The rate of VAT is changed by legislative procedure, not unilaterally by HMRC.

9   FREDERICK

The answer is C.

A is incorrect because the £10,000 of turnover will be treated as VAT inclusive. VAT of £1,666.67 (£10,000 × 1/6) will be payable.

B is incorrect as the turnover for the historic test must be measured at the end of a month.

D is incorrect as some businesses (e.g. ones making zero rated supplies) have monthly returns and under the annual accounting scheme businesses just have one yearly return.

10   PICARD

The answer is C.

Working: Cumulative taxable turnover for the last 12 months

		£
End Dec 20X5	(£5,000 × 12)	60,000
End Jan 20X6	(£60,000 + £5,600 Jan X6 – £5,000 Jan X5))	60,600
End Feb 20X6	(£60,600 + £10,100 Feb X6 – £5,000 Feb X5)	65,700
End Mar 20X6	(£65,700 + £10,200 Mar X6 – £5,000 Mar X5)	70,900
End April 20X6	(£70,900 + £11,500 Apr X6 – £5,000 Apr X5)	77,400

Tutorial note

The historic registration test is based on a business achieving £77,000 of taxable turnover in the last 12 months or since starting in business if this is less than 12 months. Taxable turnover excludes exempt supplies but includes zero rated supplies.

VAT DOCUMENTATION

11   NAASIR

(a)   The answer is C

(b)   The answer is B

(c)   The answer is B

Tutorial note

The basic tax point is the date of delivery of goods or the date of performance of services. This is the case with (c).

However, if goods or services are paid for in advance or a tax invoice is issued in advance, the date of payment or the invoice date becomes the tax point date. This is the case with (b). The tax point date is the date payment is received. Note that a proforma invoice is raised before the payment date, however a proforma invoice is not a VAT invoice. Even if a valid VAT invoice had been raised on 17 August, it was not sent to the customer until after the goods were delivered. To issue a VAT invoice it must be sent to, or given to, the customer for them to keep. A tax point cannot be created simply by preparing an invoice.

Where goods are not paid for or invoiced in advance, a later tax point can arise if a tax invoice is raised within 14 days after the basic tax point. This is the case with (a). This is referred to as the '14 day rule'.

Taxpayers can also apply to HMRC for a tax point date to fit in with their invoicing routine.

Key answer tips

Information about this topic is included in the VAT reference material provided in the real assessment, so you do not need to learn it.

However you need to be familiar with its location and content – why not look at it now?

12 AIDAN

(a)

	True	False
The tax point date is 10 July.	√	
The tax point date is 15 July.		√
An invoice for a wholly zero rated supply is not a tax invoice.	√	
Input tax recovery in respect of zero rated supplies is restricted		√

Tutorial note

An invoice for a wholly zero rated supply within the UK is not a tax invoice. Hence the 14 day rule cannot apply. The tax point date will be the earlier of the receipt of cash or the despatch of goods.

*However, zero rated supplies **are** taxable supplies and any input tax incurred in helping to make zero rated goods or perform zero rated services is fully recoverable.*

Key answer tips

Information about this topic is included in the VAT reference material provided in the real assessment, so you do not need to learn it.

However you need to be familiar with its location and content – why not look at it now?

(b)   The answer is C.

It is not a valid simplified invoice as the value of the supply exceeds £250. There is insufficient detail for it to be a valid full invoice.

13   CIARAN

Deposit paid	Goods delivered	Invoice raised	Balance paid	Tax point for deposit	Tax point for balance
28 June	14 July	17 July	5 August	28 June	17 July (14 day rule)
19 October	31 October	16 November	12 December	19 October	31 October (Delivery date)
2 December	4 December	22 December	10 December	2 December	4 December (Delivery date)

Tutorial note

The basic tax point is the date of delivery of goods or the date of performance of services.

However, if goods or services are paid for in advance or a tax invoice is issued in advance, the date of payment or the invoice date becomes the tax point date. If a part payment such as a deposit is paid in advance then there will be two tax points, one for the deposit and one for the balance of the supply.

Where goods are not paid for or invoiced in advance, a later tax point can arise if a tax invoice is raised within 14 days after the basic tax point. This is referred to as the '14 day rule'.

Key answer tips

Information about this topic is included in the VAT reference material provided in the real assessment, so you do not need to learn it.

However you need to be familiar with its location and content – why not look at it now?

14   ELIZABETH

(a)   The answer is D.

A supplier credit note means a purchase credit note. VAT on purchase credit notes is deducted from input VAT on purchase invoices so input tax will decrease.

(b)   The answer is B.

Sales to EU VAT registered customers are zero rated so there will be no effect on VAT.

15   ULRIKA

(a)   The answer is C.

(b)   The answer is D.

Key answer tips

Information about this topic is included in the VAT reference material provided in the real assessment, so you do not need to learn it.

However you need to be familiar with its location and content – why not look at it now?

16   AHMED

	Required	Not required
Time of supply	√	
Customer order number		√
Description of the type of supply	√	
Rate of VAT applicable	√	
General terms of trade		√
Any discount offered	√	
Total amount payable excluding VAT	√	
Total amount of VAT payable	√	
Acceptable methods of payment		√

Tutorial note

VAT invoices should contain the following:

1   *Identifying number which must follow a sequence*

2   *Date of supply (or tax point) and the date of issue of the invoice*

3   *Supplier's name and address and registration number*

4   *Name and address of customer, i.e. the person to whom the goods or services are supplied*

5   *Type of supply (e.g. sale, hire purchase, exchange etc.)*

6   *Description of the goods or service*

7   *Quantity of goods or extent of service*

8   *Rate of tax and amount payable (in sterling) excluding VAT for each separate description*

9   *Total amount payable (excluding VAT) in sterling*

10   *Rate of any cash discount offered (these are also called settlement discounts)*

11   *Separate rate and amount of VAT charged for each rate of VAT*

12   *Total amount of VAT chargeable.*

Less detailed invoices need to show:

1   *Date of supply*

2   *Supplier's name and address and registration number*

3   *Description of the goods or service*

4   *Rate of tax and amount payable (in sterling) including VAT for each separate rate of VAT*

Key answer tips

Information about this topic is included in the VAT reference material provided in the real assessment, so you do not need to learn it.

However you need to be familiar with its location and content – why not look at it now?

17   NERISSA

(a)

	True	False
Proforma invoices are a way of obtaining payment before goods are despatched.	√	
The purchaser can use a proforma invoice to recover input VAT.		√
Proforma invoices must show the VAT registration number of the supplier.		√

Tutorial note

*To help with cash flow, a business may issue a **proforma invoice** which essentially is a demand for payment. Once payment is received, the business will then issue a 'live' invoice to replace the proforma.*

Because a proforma invoice does not rank as a VAT invoice the supplier is not required to pay VAT to HMRC until the 'live' invoice is issued. For this reason, the customer cannot reclaim VAT on a proforma invoice but must instead wait until the valid VAT invoice is received.

*Proforma invoices must be clearly marked with the words **'This is not a VAT invoice'**.*

(b)   £600 × 20/120 = £100

An offer to pay a customer's VAT is simply a form of discount. If the customer pays £600, this will be treated as a VAT inclusive sale.

18   CHEN

(a)   The answer is D

(b)   The answer is B

Tutorial note

Sales credit notes are deducted from sales invoices and hence reduce the amount of output tax.

A supplier credit note is a purchase credit note. It is deducted from purchase invoices and hence reduces the amount of input tax. If input tax decreases, the amount of tax due to HMRC will increase.

19   EFFIE

(a)   The answer is D.

(b)   The answer is B.

Tutorial note

Retailers selling to the public do not need to issue a tax invoice to a customer unless they request one. If a customer requests a tax invoice and the total amount (including VAT) does not exceed £250, the retailer can issue a less detailed invoice.

Retailers do not need to keep copies of less detailed invoices. This is because retailers usually determine their VAT from sales records like till rolls rather than from a sales day book listing of invoices.

Key answer tips

Information about this topic is included in the VAT reference material provided in the real assessment, so you do not need to learn it.

However you need to be familiar with its location and content – why not look at it now?

20   HEI

	True	False
Businesses must keep records of all taxable and exempt supplies made in the course of business.	√	
Taxpayers need permission from HMRC before they start keeping records electronically.		√
All businesses must keep a VAT account.	√	
The balance on the VAT account represents the VAT payable to HMRC or repayable by HMRC.	√	
Sending or receiving invoices by electronic means is permitted but paper copies must also be kept.		√
Records should normally be kept for at least 3 years before being destroyed.		√
Failure to keep records can lead to a penalty.	√	

Tutorial note

Records should be kept for 6 years. Records include purchases, purchase returns day book, sales, sales returns day book, cashbook, invoices, credit notes, delivery notes, bank statements and the VAT summary (ledger account).

Key answer tips

Information about this topic is included in the VAT reference material provided in the real assessment, so you do not need to learn it.

However you need to be familiar with its location and content – why not look at it now?

21   KYRA

(a)   The answer is C.

(b)   The answer is B.

(c)   The answer is D.

Workings

		£
(a)	Value of supply	900.00
	Less: Trade discount (£900 × 10%)	(90.00)
		810.00
	Less: Settlement discount (£810 × 2%)	(16.20)
	Amount for calculation of VAT	793.80
	VAT at 20%	158.76
(b)	Value of supply	750.00
	Less: Settlement discount (£750 × 5%)	(37.50)
	Amount for calculation of VAT	712.50
	VAT at 20%	142.50
(c)	Value of supply	240.00
	Less: Settlement discount (£240 × 8%)	(19.20)
	Amount for calculation of VAT	220.80
	VAT at 5%	11.04

Tutorial note

VAT must be calculated after taking into account all the possible discount the customer could have even if the customer does not take the discount. In (b) above, where there are two rates of settlement discount, the higher must be used.

Key answer tips

Note that you can be asked to calculate using different rates of VAT in this type of question.

INPUT AND OUTPUT TAX

22   FABRIZIO

The answer is D.

Both standard rated and zero rated supplies are taxable supplies. If no exempt supplies are made then the business can recover all their input tax.

23   ROCCO

The answer is B.

Input VAT can be reclaimed on the staff entertaining and the van.

Total supplies on which VAT can be recovered £8,930 (£705 + £8,225)

This is a VAT inclusive total so the VAT included is £1,488.33 (£8,930 × 20/120)

24   VINCENZO

Description	Net £	VAT £	Gross £	Reclaim input VAT?
Repairs to property	1,900.00	380.00	2,280.00	**Yes**
Delivery van	10,000.00	2,000.00	12,000.00	**Yes**
UK Customer entertaining	640.00	128.00	768.00	**No**
Overseas customer entertaining	310.00	62.00	372.00	**Yes**
Car (pool car with no private use)	8,400.00	1,680.00	10,080.00	**Yes**

Tutorial note

VAT cannot be recovered on entertaining, except for staff entertaining and entertaining overseas customers.

VAT cannot be recovered on the purchase of cars which have an element of private use.

Input VAT can be recovered on cars which are 100% used for the business, such as the pool car.

Key answer tips

Information about this topic is included in the VAT reference material provided in the real assessment, so you do not need to learn it.

However you need to be familiar with its location and content – why not look at it now?

25 CHO LTD

The answer is C.

	£
Output tax on scale charge (£282 × 20/120)	47.00
Input tax on petrol (£822.50 × 20/120)	(137.08)
Net input tax recoverable	90.08

Tutorial note

When a business provides private fuel for an employee, a VAT scale charge depending on the CO_2 emission level of the car is added to outputs and output tax is increased.

Input tax on all the fuel paid for by the business can then be recovered.

Key answer tips

Information about this topic is included in the VAT reference material provided in the real assessment, so you do not need to learn it.

However you need to be familiar with its location and content – why not look at it now

26 SOOK

The answer is C.

Tutorial note

For a partially exempt trader, input tax suffered by a business has to be split between that relating to taxable and to exempt supplies. Overhead costs which do not relate directly to taxable or exempt supplies are apportioned.

Input tax suffered on goods and services used to create exempt supplies cannot normally be recovered. However, if the de minimis limits are not exceeded, all of the input VAT can be recovered.

27   JERZY

	True	False
Traders who make only exempt supplies cannot register for VAT.	√	
Traders who only make zero rated supplies have to register for VAT.		√
Zero rated supplies made by a registered trader are not classed as taxable supplies.		√
Traders making only exempt supplies cannot recover input tax.	√	
VAT registered traders making a mix of zero rated and exempt supplies cannot recover any input tax.		√

Tutorial note

In order to register for VAT, a trader must be making or intending to make taxable supplies. Exempt supplies are not taxable supplies, so traders making only exempt supplies cannot register and cannot recover input tax.

Traders making only zero rated supplies can register, as zero rated supplies are taxable supplies. Such traders can also choose not to register if they wish to avoid the administration burden of dealing with VAT. However, they cannot reclaim input tax if they do not register.

Traders making a mix of zero rated and exempt supplies can recover a proportion of their input tax.

28   RAFA AND CO

The answer is D.

Options A, B and C mean that the business is only claiming business VAT so there is no need to account for a fuel scale charge.

Tutorial note

If a business does not want to pay a fuel scale charge then they can either:

(a)   Reclaim only VAT on business fuel (detailed records of business and private mileage needs to be kept to prove the business mileage), or

(b)   Not claim any VAT on fuel at all even for commercial vehicles. This has the advantage of being simple and is useful if mileage is low.

(c)   Only use fuel for business purposes.

Key answer tips

Information about this topic is included in the VAT reference material provided in the real assessment, so you do not need to learn it.

However you need to be familiar with its location and content – why not look at it now?

29 FINIAN

Item	Input tax recovered	Sale proceeds (excluding VAT)	Output VAT
		£	£.pp
Computer	Yes	400	80.00
Car	Yes	7,500	1,500.00
Van	Yes	6,100	1,220.00
Car	No	8,400	Nil

Tutorial note

Output tax must be charged on the sale of capital assets except for cars on which no input tax was recovered.

30 ALBERT

The answer is C.

Input VAT can be recovered on half of the entertaining costs which relate to staff and on the van. No input VAT can be recovered on non staff entertaining.

(£10,700 + (50% × £780)) × 1/6 = £1,848.33

31 VICTORIA LTD

The answer is D

Tutorial note

When a business provides private fuel for an employee, a VAT scale charge depending on the CO_2 emission level of the car is added to outputs and output tax is increased.

Input tax on all the fuel paid for by the business can then be recovered.

Key answer tips

Information about this topic is included in the VAT reference material provided in the real assessment, so you do not need to learn it.

However you need to be familiar with its location and content – why not look at it now?

32 ORSON

The answer is A.

Tutorial note

A business can reclaim the VAT according to the tax point of the purchase which is not necessarily the payment date. This is usually the date the goods/services are made available to the customer or when the invoice is issued (if that is within 14 days of delivery).

Key answer tips

Information about this topic is included in the VAT reference material provided in the real assessment, so you do not need to learn it.

However you need to be familiar with its location and content – why not look at it now?

33 MELINDA

	Recover	Cannot recover
Purchases for resale	√	
New laptop computer for Melinda's daughter		√
New desk for the business office (Melinda has lost the VAT receipt)		√
Motorcycle for business deliveries	√	

Tutorial note

In order to claim back input VAT on goods or services, the trader must have a valid VAT invoice and the items must be for business use.

34   NASHEEN

The answer is D

	£ pp
AB Ltd (£562 × 20/120)	93.66
XY plc (£750 × 20%)	150.00
	———
Total output tax	243.66
	———

35   MANINDER

The answer is B

Output VAT should be charged on the standard rated sales and on the sale of plant.

Output VAT is £9,029.00 ((£40,145 + £5,000) × 20%).

36   HARI

The answers are A and C.

Answer A is wrong because the debt must simply have been written off. There is no time limit.

Answer C is wrong. There is no requirement that the debtor should be formally insolvent, in administration or in liquidation.

Answers B and D are valid requirements.

Key answer tips

Information about this topic is included in the VAT reference material provided in the real assessment, so you do not need to learn it.

However you need to be familiar with its location and content – why not look at it now?

ACCOUNTING SCHEMES

Key answer tips

There is much Information about all accounting schemes included in the VAT reference material provided in the real assessment, so you do not need to learn it.

However you need to be familiar with its location and content – why not look at it now?

---

37   EXE LTD

(a)   The answer is C.

(b)   The answer is B.

Tutorial note

When a business makes a VAT return they have one month and 7 days from the end of the VAT period to submit the return online.

The first time that a business submits a VAT return late, they are issued with a surcharge liability notice. This lasts 12 months and if the business pays late or submits their return late in the 12 month period it is extended. A late payment during the surcharge period attracts a surcharge penalty.

38   RAVI

	True	False
VAT is normally payable at the same time that the return is due	√	
Paying VAT by direct debit gives the business an extra 5 bank working days from the normal payment date before payment is taken from the account.		√
New businesses have a choice about whether they submit returns electronically or on paper.		√
Quarterly VAT returns are all made up to 30 April, 31 July, 31 October and 31 January		√

Tutorial note

VAT payments are due at the same time as the return. Funds must clear HMRC bank account within 1 month and 7 days of the end of the VAT return period.

Direct debit payments are taken from the business bank account 3 bank working days from the normal payment date.

All new businesses have to use electronic returns. There is no choice.

There are three sets of quarterly return dates. HMRC allocate businesses to one of these to spread out the flow of returns submitted.

39   ANNUAL ACCOUNTING

(a)   The answer is C.

(b)   The answer is B.

(c)   The answer is B.

(d)   The answer is B.

Key answer tips

Note that this can be answered by looking in the reference material provided in the real assessment.

Tutorial note

The annual accounting scheme allows businesses to submit one VAT return each year. This is due two months after the year end. No seven day extension is allowed for electronic filing.

The scheme is not suitable for businesses which make zero rated supplies. This is because such businesses can normally claim regular repayments of input tax as they have no output tax to pay over. If they choose annual accounting, they will only get one repayment per year.

VAT payments on account have to be made throughout the year. VAT is not just paid once a year with the return. These payments on account are based on last year's VAT liability. If a business has a reducing turnover of taxable supplies it will not benefit them to join the annual accounting scheme. This is because they will be making payments on account based on last year's higher VAT liability. If they used the normal accounting scheme they would be paying lower VAT payments based on the current year's liability.

40   ZED LTD

The answer is C.

Payments on account are 10% of last year's liability. This is £7,290. Nine monthly payments are made at the end of months 4 to 12 in the accounting period.

41 TARAN

	True	False
Taxpayers must be up to date with their VAT returns before they are allowed to join the scheme.	√	
Monthly payments on account are 10% of the previous year's VAT liability.	√	
Monthly payments can be made using any method convenient to the taxpayer.		√
Monthly payments are made 7 days after the end of months 2 to 10 in the accounting period.		√
The scheme allows businesses to budget for their VAT payments more easily.	√	

Tutorial note

Payments must be made electronically with no extra 7 days allowed.

Payments are made at the end of months 4 to 12 during the accounting period not 2 to 10.

42 ARTHUR

Answers A and D are correct.

B is incorrect as traders can only join the scheme provided their annual taxable turnover does not exceed £1,350,000.

C is incorrect as VAT invoices still have to be sent to customers.

43 LAREDO

The answer is D.

Tutorial note

With the cash accounting scheme, the tax point date is the date the payment is received.

44   CASH ACCOUNTING

	Will benefit	Will not benefit
A manufacturing business that sells all its output on credit to other businesses. Debtors take on average 45 days to pay. The business aims to pay creditors within 30 days of receiving purchase invoices.	√	
A clothes shop based in a town centre which sells standard rated supplies to members of the public for cash.		√
A wholesaler who sells to other businesses on 40 days credit. In the last 12 months the business has suffered a steep rise in bad debts.	√	
A business making solely zero rated supplies to other businesses.		√

Tutorial note

The cash accounting scheme allows businesses to pay over output tax when customers pay and reclaim input tax when creditors are paid. Output and input VAT totals are taken from the cash book.

The first business will benefit from the cash accounting scheme because they sell all their goods on credit. They will not have to pay over output VAT until their debtors pay. Under the normal accounting scheme they would have to pay over output VAT before receiving cash from customers. There is a disadvantage because the business cannot reclaim input VAT until they pay for the goods but overall they should benefit.

The second business sells all its goods for cash, so adopting the cash accounting scheme makes no difference to the time they have to account for output VAT. However, with cash accounting the business cannot reclaim input VAT until they pay creditors. This will delay the recovery of input VAT compared to the normal method.

The third business will benefit because with cash accounting there is no problem of bad debts from a VAT point of view. Using the normal accounting method a business must pay over VAT according to the normal tax point rules. This is usually before receiving cash from the customer. If the customer never pays up then the business can claim back the output VAT paid over but not until at least 6 months have passed. This is a cash flow disadvantage for the business which does not happen with cash accounting.

The fourth business makes zero rated supplies so has no output tax to pay over. However it can reclaim its input VAT, usually on a monthly basis. The business will not benefit from cash accounting because it would delay the time at which they could reclaim input tax.

45   FLAT RATE SCHEME

	Will benefit	Will not benefit
A business making solely zero rated supplies to other businesses.		√
A business with a lower than average (for their trade sector) level of input tax.	√	
A business with a higher level of standard rated supplies than other businesses in the same trade sector.	√	

Tutorial note

When using the flat rate scheme, businesses calculate how much VAT to pay over to HMRC by using a fixed percentage of their VAT inclusive total turnover (including exempt supplies).

If a business makes wholly zero rated supplies their output VAT is nil and instead of having to pay over VAT they can reclaim the input tax they have paid. With the flat rate scheme they would have to pay over VAT instead of reclaiming it.

The flat rate percentage used by a business is fixed by reference to the average outputs less inputs for a typical business in that particular trade sector. If a business has lower than average inputs and hence input tax, they would benefit from using the flat rate scheme. Their overall VAT bill would be based on the higher trade sector proportion of inputs rather than their own lower figure.

The same logic would apply to the third business which has a higher level of standard rated supplies. The trade percentage used in the flat rate scheme would be based on a lower average of taxable outputs and hence should produce less tax than using normal VAT accounting.

46   RAY

	True	False
A business can join the flat rate scheme provided their taxable turnover for the next 12 months is expected to be less than £230,000.		√
VAT due to HMRC is calculated as a fixed percentage of VAT inclusive taxable turnovers.		√
VAT invoices must still be issued.	√	
A business can be in both the flat rate scheme and the annual accounting scheme at the same time.	√	
The scheme cuts down on the time spent on VAT administration.	√	
Businesses cannot pay less VAT under the flat rate scheme than the normal method of accounting for VAT.		√

Tutorial note

A business can join the flat rate scheme provided their taxable turnover (excluding VAT) is less than £150,000. They have to leave the scheme when their total turnover exceeds £230,000 (including VAT and exempt supplies.)

The VAT calculation is based on VAT inclusive TOTAL turnover, not just taxable turnover.

It is possible for a business to pay less VAT under the flat rate scheme than under the normal accounting scheme.

47   FENFANG

The answer is C.

VAT is calculated as 8% of £28,080 (£22,470 + £4,500 + £1,110) = £2,246.40.

ERRORS AND PENALTIES

48   VAT PENALTIES

	True	False
Tax avoidance is a criminal offence and means using illegal means to reduce tax liability.		√
A penalty can be charged if a trader fails to register at the correct time.	√	
A registered trader who makes an error on a return leading to underpayment of tax will always be charged a penalty.		√
If a registered trader does not submit a VAT return then HMRC can issue an assessment to collect VAT due.	√	

Tutorial note

The description given is of tax evasion. Tax avoidance means using lawful means to reduce your tax liability.

A penalty can be charged if a business does not register on time.

If an error is neither careless nor deliberate and the trader takes steps to correct it, then they may not be charged a penalty.

If a trader does not submit their VAT return then HMRC can issue an assessment showing the amount HMRC believes is due based on their best estimate.

49 VAT ERRORS

(a)

	Net error £	Turnover £	Include in next return	Separate disclosure
1	24,567	2,000,000		√
2	4,568	85,400	√	
3	35,980	4,567,090	√	
4	51,600	10,000,000		√

Tutorial note

When a trader discovers a VAT error they must inform HMRC. If the net error is less than a certain limit and is not deliberate, it can be included on the next VAT return. If not, it must be disclosed separately on Form VAT 652 or in a letter.

The limit operates as follows:

Net errors up to £10,000 can always be included on the next VAT return.

Net errors above £50,000 must always be separately disclosed.

Errors between these limits can be included on the next VAT return if they are no more than 1% of turnover (specifically the figure in Box 6 of the return).

(b)   Net error £41.86

	£
Output tax reduced by (£81 – £18)	63.00
Input tax reduced by	(21.14)
	41.86

This will reduce VAT due.

Key answer tips

Information about this topic is included in the VAT reference material provided in the real assessment, so you do not need to learn it.

However you need to be familiar with its location and content – why not look at it now?

50   DEFAULT SURCHARGE

(a)

	True	False
A default only occurs when a business pays its VAT late.		√
A surcharge liability notice lasts for 6 months from the end of the period of default.		√
Once a trader has received a surcharge liability notice, he must keep all his returns and payments up to date for the period of the surcharge notice, otherwise it will be extended.	√	

Tutorial note

A default under the default surcharge scheme occurs when a trader files their VAT return late or pays its VAT late.

A surcharge liability notice lasts for 12 months not 6 months.

If the trader defaults again during the surcharge period they will have their surcharge period extended to 12 months after the end of the new period of default. If the default is a late payment they may also have to pay a penalty. Hence it is true to say that a business must 'keep out of trouble' for 12 months by paying VAT and submitting returns on time otherwise their surcharge period will be extended.

(b)   The answer is B

The VAT due in the VAT control account is £2,485.40 too high. This will occur if there are either too few debits or too many credits. Answer A would result in too many debits and hence a lower balance in the control account.

PREPARING A VAT RETURN AND COMMUNICATING VAT INFORMATION

VAT RETURNS AND COMMUNICATIONS

51 PATEL

Bad debt relief can be claimed on the debts of £4,200 and £6,552 only.

The amount claimed is £1,792 = (£4,200 + £6,552) × 20/120.

No relief can be claimed on the debts of £7,000 and £2,500 as the end of the quarter (i.e. 30 September X1) is not 6 months since the later of:

- the date of supply or
- the date payment was due.

Tutorial note

Unless a business uses a special accounting scheme, output tax is due at the normal tax point date. This will usually be before the debtor has paid. If the debtor never pays up then the business can claim back the output VAT paid over on the sale provided the following conditions are met:

(i)   Output VAT on the original invoice has been paid over.

(ii) Six months have elapsed since the later of the date of supply or the date payment was due.

(iii) The debt has been written off as irrecoverable in the financial accounting records.

The VAT on the bad debt is included in Box 4 on the VAT return.

Key answer tips

Information about this topic is included in the VAT reference material provided in the real assessment, so you do not need to learn it.

However you need to be familiar with its location and content – why not look at it now?

52 DAVIES LTD

VAT return to 31 May 20X2

		£
VAT due in this period on **sales** and other outputs	Box 1	88,164.00
VAT due in this period on **acquisitions** from other **EC Member States**	Box 2	0.00
Total VAT due (**the sum of boxes 1 and 2**)	Box 3	88,164.00
VAT reclaimed in the period on **purchases** and other inputs, including acquisitions from the EC	Box 4	34,493.05
Net VAT to be paid to HM Revenue & Customs or reclaimed by you (**Difference between boxes 3 and 4**)	Box 5	53,670.95
Total value of **sales** and all other outputs excluding any VAT. **Include your box 8 figure**	Box 6	600,160
Total value of purchases and all other inputs excluding any VAT. **Include your box 9 figure**	Box 7	199,720
Total value of all **supplies** of goods and related costs, excluding any VAT, to other **EC Member States**	Box 8	107,240
Total value of all **acquisitions** of goods and related costs, excluding any VAT, from other **EC Member States**	Box 9	0

Workings

	£.pp
Box 1 – Output tax	
March	24,200.00
April	35,804.00
May	28,160.00
	————
	88,164.00
	————

		£.pp
Box 4 – Input tax		
March		13,840.00
April		12,636.00
May		13,468.00
Less: Input tax over claim		(5,450.95)
		————
		34,493.05
		————
		£
Box 6 – Total outputs		
UK sales (£121,000 + £179,020 + £140,800)		440,820
EU sales (£30,300 + £41,160 + £35,780)		107,240
Exports (£17,000 + £14,900 + £20,200)		52,100
		————
		600,160
		————
Box 7 – Total inputs		
March		69,200
April		63,180
May		67,340
		————
		199,720
		————

Tutorial note

1 Purchases and sales figures extracted from ledgers will always be net of VAT.

2 Export sales are dealt with as follows:

Sales to registered businesses in the EU are zero rated so there is no output VAT to include in Box 1. The sales are part of the total outputs included in Box 6 and are also entered in Box 8.

Sales to non registered customers in the EU are treated just like normal UK sales and are not included in Box 8.

Sales to customers outside the EU are zero rated and they only appear on the VAT return as part of the outputs in Box 6.

Key answer tips

Information about this topic is included in the VAT reference material provided in the real assessment, so you do not need to learn it.

However you need to be familiar with its location and content – why not look at it now?

53   DHONI LTD

Email	
To:	Financial Accountant
From:	Accounting technician
Date:	17 January 20X3
Subject:	VAT error

An error occurred in the VAT return for the previous quarter. Output VAT of £4,672.90 was **understated.** This resulted in VAT being **underpaid.**

This error **was included on the VAT return to 31 December.**

Kind regards

Tutorial note

When a trader discovers a VAT error they must inform HMRC. If the net error is less than a certain limit and is not deliberate it can be included on the next VAT return. If not, it must be disclosed separately on Form VAT 652 or in a letter.

The limit operates as follows:

- *Net errors up to £10,000 can always be included on the next VAT return.*

- *Net errors above £50,000 must always be separately disclosed.*

Errors between these limits can be included on the next VAT return if they are no more than 1% of turnover (specifically the figure in Box 6 of the return).

Key answer tips

Information about this topic is included in the VAT reference material provided in the real assessment, so you do not need to learn it.

However you need to be familiar with its location and content – why not look at it now?

---

54   JASPER

		£
VAT due in this period on **acquisitions** from other **EC Member States**	**Box 2**	5,480.00
VAT reclaimed in the period on **purchases** and other inputs, including acquisitions from the EC	**Box 4**	23,960.00
Total value of purchases and all other inputs excluding any VAT. **Include your box 9 figure**	**Box 7**	119,800
Total value of all **acquisitions** of goods and related costs, excluding any VAT, from other **EC Member States**	**Box 9**	27,400

Workings

Box 2	VAT on acquisitions from other EU countries	
	20% × £27,400	£5,480.00
Box 4	VAT reclaimed	
	20% × (£54,800 + £27,400 + £37,600)	£23,960.00
Box 7	Total purchases	
	(£54,800 + £27,400 + £37,600)	£119,800
Box 9	Purchases from other EU countries	£27,400

Tutorial note

Purchases (acquisitions) from EU businesses are dealt with as follows:

- *The business must account for both output and input VAT.*

- *The VAT on these purchases is included in Box 2 and then again as part of the input VAT in Box 4.*

The net value of the purchases is included in the inputs in Box 7 and again in Box 9.

Key answer tips

Information about this topic is included in the VAT reference material provided in the real assessment, so you do not need to learn it.

However you need to be familiar with its location and content – why not look at it now?

55 TROTT

VAT return to 31 March 20X5

		£
VAT due in this period on **sales** and other outputs	**Box 1**	1,452.00
VAT due in this period on **acquisitions** from other **EC Member States**	**Box 2**	0.00
Total VAT due (**the sum of boxes 1 and 2**)	**Box 3**	1,452.00
VAT reclaimed in the period on **purchases** and other inputs, including acquisitions from the EC	**Box 4**	824.16
Net VAT to be paid to HM Revenue & Customs or reclaimed by you (**Difference between boxes 3 and 4**)	**Box 5**	627.84
Total value of **sales** and all other outputs excluding any VAT. **Include your box 8 figure**	**Box 6**	7,260
Total value of purchases and all other inputs excluding any VAT. **Include your box 9 figure**	**Box 7**	3,925
Total value of all **supplies** of goods and related costs, excluding any VAT, to other **EC Member States**	**Box 8**	0
Total value of all **acquisitions** of goods and related costs, excluding any VAT, from other **EC Member States**	**Box 9**	0

Workings

	£.pp
Box 1 – Output tax	
Sales day book	1,470.00
Cash receipts book	52.00
	_____
	1,522.00
Less: Sales credit note day book	(70.00)
	_____
	1,452.00
	_____

		£.pp
Box 4 – Input tax		
	Purchase day book	722.00
	Cash payments book	30.00
	Petty cash book	33.00
	Bad debt relief (£235 × 20/120)	39.16
		824.16

		£
Box 6 – Total outputs		
	Sales day book	7,350
	Cash receipts book	260
		7,610
	Less: Sales credit note day book	(350)
		7,260
Box 7 – Total inputs		
	Purchase day book (£2,160 + £1,450)	3,610
	Cash payments book	150
	Petty cash book	165
		3,925

Tutorial note

1   *Unless a business uses a special accounting scheme, output tax is due at the normal tax point date. This will usually be before the debtor has paid. If the debtor never pays up then the business can claim back the output VAT paid over on the sale provided the following conditions are met:*

(i)   *Output VAT on the original invoice has been paid over.*

(ii)   *Six months have elapsed since the later of the date of supply or the date payment was due.*

(iii)   *The debt has been written off as irrecoverable in the financial accounting records.*

The VAT on the bad debt is included in Box 4.

2   *When you are given figures from cash receipt or payment books you are not interested in the amounts received from debtors or paid to creditors, unless the business uses the cash accounting scheme.*

The information we need from cash books (including petty cash books) is the amount of any cash purchases and expenses, and any cash sales, plus the related VAT.

The VAT on credit sales and purchases is taken from the daybooks.

Sales credit notes are deducted from sales for Box 6 and the VAT on sales credit notes is deducted from the output tax in Box 1.

56   BELL

Email	
To:	Bell
From:	Accounting technician
Date:	17 April 20X5
Subject:	Bad debt relief

Thank you for advising me about the debt you wrote off. I have included relief for this in the VAT return for the quarter ended *31 March 20X5*.

Relief can be claimed because the debt was due for payment more than **6 months** ago.

The **output** tax paid on the original invoice can be reclaimed by including the amount in **Box 4.** The amount of bad debt relief is £*1,077.83*.

Kind regards

Key answer tips

Information about this topic is included in the VAT reference material provided in the real assessment, so you do not need to learn it.

However you need to be familiar with its location and content – why not look at it now

---

57   MISTRY

(a)   Calculate the figure for Box 2 of the VAT return – VAT due on acquisitions from other EC member states

£3,000.00

(b)   Calculate the figure for Box 1 of the VAT return – VAT due on sales and other outputs

£132,200.00

(c)   Calculate the figure for box 4 of the VAT return – VAT reclaimed on purchases and other inputs, including acquisitions from the EC

£65,200.00

Workings

(a)   (£15,000.00 × 20%) = £3,000.00

(b)   (£134,000.00 – £1,800.00) = £132,200.00

(c)   (£62,200 + £3,000) = £65,200.00

Key answer tips

Information about this topic is included in the VAT reference material provided in the real assessment, so you do not need to learn it.

However you need to be familiar with its location and content – why not look at it now?

---

58   **BARTLET LTD**

VAT return for the quarter ended 30 September 20X2

		£
VAT due in this period on **sales** and other outputs	**Box 1**	4,340.00
VAT due in this period on **acquisitions** from other **EC Member States**	**Box 2**	572.00
Total VAT due (**the sum of boxes 1 and 2**)	**Box 3**	4,912.00
VAT reclaimed in the period on **purchases** and other inputs, including acquisitions from the EC	**Box 4**	4,100.00
Net VAT to be paid to HM Revenue & Customs or reclaimed by you (**Difference between boxes 3 and 4**)	**Box 5**	812.00
Total value of **sales** and all other outputs excluding any VAT. **Include your box 8 figure**	**Box 6**	45,675
Total value of purchases and all other inputs excluding any VAT. **Include your box 9 figure**	**Box 7**	20,500
Total value of all **supplies** of goods and related costs, excluding any VAT, to other **EC Member States**	**Box 8**	5,105
Total value of all **acquisitions** of goods and related costs, excluding any VAT, from other **EC Member States**	**Box 9**	2,860

Workings

	£.pp
Box 1 – Output tax	
On UK standard rated sales	4,100.00
On sales to EU non registered customers	240.00
	————
	4,340.00
	————
Box 4 – Input tax	
On UK purchases and expenses	3,400.00
Purchases from EU businesses	572.00
Petty cash book	128.00
	————
	4,100.00
	————

	£
Box 6 – Total outputs	
UK standard rated sales	20,500
UK zero rated sales	13,470
UK exempt sales	1,650
Sales to VAT registered EU customers	5,105
Sales to non VAT registered EU customers	1,200
Exports outside the EU	3,750
	————
	45,675
	————
Box 7 – Total inputs	
UK purchases and expenses	17,000
Purchases from EU businesses	2,860
Petty cash purchases and expenses	640
	————
	20,500
	————

Tutorial note

1   Export sales are dealt with as follows:

Sales to registered businesses in the EU are zero rated so there is no output VAT to include in Box 1. The sales are part of the total outputs included in Box 6 and are also entered in Box 8.

Sales to non registered customers in the EU are treated just like normal UK sales and are not included in Box 8.

Sales to customers outside the EU are zero rated and they only appear on the VAT return as part of the outputs in Box 6.

2   *Purchases (acquisitions) from EU businesses are dealt with as follows:*

The business must account for both output and input VAT.

The VAT on these purchases is included in Box 2 and then again as part of the input VAT in Box 4.

The net value of the purchases is included in the inputs in Box 7 and again in Box 9.

3   *Exempt sales must be included as part of the outputs in Box 6.*

4   *Wages are outside the scope of VAT and are not included on the VAT return.*

Key answer tips

Information about accounting for overseas sales and purchases is included in the VAT reference material provided in the real assessment, so you do not need to learn it.

However you need to be familiar with its location and content – why not look at it now?

59   SEABORN LTD

Email

To: Financial Accountant

From: Accounting Technician

Date: 5 September 20X6

Subject: Filing VAT returns

VAT returns must be submitted **quarterly** unless you are a net repayment trader when returns can be made **monthly.**

Returns must be filed within **1 month** after the end of the VAT period with an extension of **7 days** where returns are filed online.

You **must file online.**

Kind regards

Key answer tips

Information about this topic is included in the VAT reference material provided in the real assessment, so you do not need to learn it.

However you need to be familiar with its location and content – why not look at it now?

60   KEIKO LTD

The VAT due is £2,076.66

	£
Cash sales receipts	780
Receipts from debtors	39,745
	40,525
Less: Cash paid to creditors	(27,890)
Petty cash purchases	(175)
	12,460
VAT at 20/120	2,076.66

Tutorial note

When a business uses cash accounting, the relevant figures for VAT are taken from cash receipts and payments rather than from invoiced amounts.

Note that the layout above is not intended to represent a VAT account or VAT return. It is just a working to calculate VAT due.

61   O'BRIEN

VAT return for the quarter ended 30 June 20X2

		£
VAT due in this period on **sales** and other outputs	**Box 1**	14,908.84
VAT due in this period on **acquisitions** from other **EC Member States**	**Box 2**	0.00
Total VAT due (**the sum of boxes 1 and 2**)	**Box 3**	14,908.84
VAT reclaimed in the period on **purchases** and other inputs, including acquisitions from the EC	**Box 4**	17,655.16
Net VAT to be paid to HM Revenue & Customs or reclaimed by you (**Difference between boxes 3 and 4**)	**Box 5**	−2,746.32
Total value of **sales** and all other outputs excluding any VAT. **Include your box 8 figure**	**Box 6**	148,941

Total value of purchases and all other inputs excluding any VAT. **Include your box 9 figure**	**Box 7**	88,276
Total value of all **supplies** of goods and related costs, excluding any VAT, to other **EC Member States**	**Box 8**	17,250
Total value of all **acquisitions** of goods and related costs, excluding any VAT, from other **EC Member States**	**Box 9**	0

Workings

	£.pp
Box 1 – Output tax	
From sales day book	5,974.41
From cash receipts book	780.10
Output tax understated on last return	8,100.00
VAT fuel scale charge (£326 × 20/120)	54.33
	14,908.84
Box 4 – Input tax	
From purchase day book	17,435.26
From cash payments book	219.90
	17,655.16

	£
Box 6 – Total outputs	
Sales day book total less VAT (£150,743.61 – £5,974.41)	144,769.20
Cash sales	3,900.50
VAT fuel scale charge (£326 – £54.33)	271.67
	148,941.37
Box 7 – Total inputs	
Purchase day book total less VAT (£104,611.58 – £17,435.26)	87,176.32
Cash purchases	1,099.50
	88,275.82

Tutorial note

1   *When a trader discovers a VAT error they must inform HMRC. If the net error is less than a certain limit and is non careless and non deliberate it can be included on the next VAT return. If not, it must be disclosed separately on Form VAT 652 or in a letter.*

The limit operates as follows:

Net errors up to £10,000 can always be included on the next VAT return.

Net errors above £50,000 must always be separately disclosed.

Errors between these limits can be included on the next VAT return if they are no more than 1% of turnover (specifically the figure in Box 6 of the return).

2   *When you are given figures from cash receipt or payment books you are not interested in the amounts received from debtors or paid to creditors, unless the business uses the cash accounting scheme. The information we need from cash books (including petty cash books) is the amount of any cash purchases and expenses, and any cash sales, plus the related VAT.*

The VAT on credit sales and purchases is taken from the daybooks.

3   *Export sales are dealt with as follows:*

Sales to registered businesses in the EU are zero rated so there is no output VAT to include in Box 1. The sales are part of the total outputs included in Box 6 and are also entered in Box 8.

Sales to non registered customers in the EU are treated just like normal UK sales and are not included in Box 8.

Sales to customers outside the EU are zero rated and they only appear on the VAT return as part of the outputs in Box 6.

4   *When a business reclaims input VAT on petrol or diesel consumed in a car which has both business and private use, then a VAT scale charge must be used to increase outputs and output tax. The scale charges vary with the engine size of the car and the figures are given VAT inclusive.*

Key answer tips

Information about these topics is included in the VAT reference material provided in the real assessment, so you do not need to learn it.

However you need to be familiar with its location and content – why not look at it now?

62   MILES

Email

To: Miles

From: Accounting technician

Date: 14 July 20X2

Subject: VAT and cars

Input VAT on the purchase of a car for both business and private use **cannot** be recovered.

Generally input VAT on all car running costs can be recovered but only if you account for a VAT scale charge.

The VAT exclusive element of this charge is **added to inputs in Box 6.**

The VAT element of the charge is **added to output tax in Box 1.**

If you do not wish to account for a VAT fuel charge you can **reclaim only 80% of your input VAT.**

Kind regards

Key answer tips

Information about this topic is included in the VAT reference material provided in the real assessment, so you do not need to learn it.

---

63   SPRINGER

The answer is £3,775.00.

Workings

	£
Sales invoices issued	67,800
Cash sales receipts	235
Purchase debit notes issued	2,100
	70,135
Less: Purchase invoices	(45,350)
Petty cash purchases	(155)
Sales credit notes	(1,980)
	22,650
VAT at 20/120	3,775.00

Tutorial note

If a buyer returns goods to their supplier they have three options:

1   *Return their original invoice and receive a replacement invoice with the correct amount of VAT.*

2   *Obtain a credit note from the supplier.*

3   *Issue a debit note to their supplier*

A purchase credit or debit note reduces input VAT that the business can reclaim.

From the point of view of the supplier a debit note received or a sales credit note issued will reduce output VAT.

Note that the layout above is not intended to represent a VAT account or VAT return. It is just a working to calculate VAT due.

64   STEWART LTD (1)

VAT return to 31 October 20X5

		£
VAT due in this period on **sales** and other outputs	Box 1	28,376.61
VAT due in this period on **acquisitions** from other **EC Member States**	Box 2	2,918.60
Total VAT due (**the sum of boxes 1 and 2**)	Box 3	31,295.21
VAT reclaimed in the period on **purchases** and other inputs, including acquisitions from the EC	Box 4	22,227.80
Net VAT to be paid to HM Revenue & Customs or reclaimed by you (**Difference between boxes 3 and 4**)	Box 5	9,067.41
Total value of **sales** and all other outputs excluding any VAT. **Include your box 8 figure**	Box 6	141,882
Total value of purchases and all other inputs excluding any VAT. **Include your box 9 figure**	Box 7	111,139
Total value of all **supplies** of goods and related costs, excluding any VAT, to other **EC Member States**	Box 8	0
Total value of all **acquisitions** of goods and related costs, excluding any VAT, from other **EC Member States**	Box 9	14,593

Workings

	£.pp
Box 1 – Output tax	
Per the ledger	28,376.61
Box 2 – VAT due on acquisitions from other EC states	
Purchases from EC businesses (£14,593 × 20%)	2,918.60
Box 4 – Input tax	
On UK purchases and expenses	15,309.20
Purchases from EC businesses	2,918.60
VAT on purchase of lorry	4,000.00
	22,227.80

	£
Box 6 – Total outputs	
UK sales	145,450
Less: Credit notes	(3,568)
	141,882
Box 7 – Total inputs	
UK purchases	59,678
Expenses	19,437
Purchases from EC businesses	14,593
Purchase of lorry	20,000
Less: Purchase credit notes	(2,569)
	111,139

Tutorial note

1   *Purchases and sales figures extracted from ledgers will always be net of VAT.*

2   *Purchases (acquisitions) from EU businesses are dealt with as follows:*

The business must account for both output and input VAT.

The VAT on these purchases is included in Box 2 and then again as part of the input VAT in Box 4.

The net value of the purchases is included in the inputs in Box 7 and again in Box 9.

3   *Wages are outside the scope of VAT and are not included on the VAT return.*

Key answer tips

Information about EU sales and purchases and VAT on motor expenses, is included in the VAT reference material provided in the real assessment, so you do not need to learn it.

However you need to be familiar with its location and content – why not look at it now?

65   STEWART LTD (2)

To: Financial accountant

From: Accounting technician

Date: 17 November 20X5

Subject: VAT return and capital expenditure

Please be advised that I have just completed the VAT return for the quarter ended **31 October 20X5**.

The amount of VAT **payable** will be £9,067.41.

The return must be with HMRC on or before **7 December 20X5**.

The VAT will be **paid electronically by 7 December 20X5.**

I have included the invoice for capital expenditure. VAT of **£4,000** can be reclaimed on this expenditure.

Kind regards

Section 3

MOCK ASSESSMENT QUESTIONS

SECTION 1

TASK 1.1

Are the following statements true or false?

Tick the correct box for each statement.

	True	False
A business has an expected turnover for the next 12 months of £85,000 but they sell goods that are zero-rated so they cannot register for VAT.		✓
A business has prepared their VAT return for the quarter ended 31 March 20X2; they must pay by electronic transfer by 30 April 20X2.		✓
Tax evasion is illegal.	✓	

TASK 1.2

(a)   A business sells goods at the standard rate of 20%. The goods are sold for £560 excluding VAT. A settlement discount of 5% is offered if the customer pays within 7 days and 2.5% settlement discount is offered if the customer pays within 14 days.

What is the amount of VAT that would be shown on the sales invoice?

A   £109.20

B   £106.40

C   £112.00

D   £103.60

(b)   If you send a sales credit note to a customer for £40 plus standard rate VAT, what effect does this have on the amount of VAT payable to HMRC by your business?

A   The amount payable will decrease by £40

B   The amount payable will increase by £40

C   The amount payable will decrease by £8

D   The amount payable will increase by £8

TASK 1.3

(a) State whether input VAT can be reclaimed on each of the purchases below. All purchases are made by a business for business purposes. The car is used by the managing director for both business and private mileage.

Item	Net £	VAT £	Gross £	Reclaim?
Motor car	2,500.00	500.00	3,000.00	No
Stationery	25.00	5.00	30.00	Yes
Fixtures and fittings	1,212.00	242.40	1,454.40	Yes
Staff entertaining	250.00	50.00	300.00	Yes
Printer	65.00	13.00	78.00	Yes

(b) A business makes a purchase of materials which are delivered on 12 May 20X2. The invoice was issued on 10 May 20X2 but had already been paid on 25 April 20X2.

What is the actual tax point for this purchase?

A   25 April 20X2

B   10 May 20X2

C   12 May 20X2

D   26 May 20X2

TASK 1.4

(a) Which of the following is an advantage of the annual accounting scheme?

A   It is good for businesses that are experiencing a decrease in turnover compared to previous years

B   It is beneficial for businesses that have a repayment due to them rather than having to make a payment of VAT

C   It reduces the amount of administration work to be completed

(b) Jasper Enterprises uses the annual accounting scheme. Their annual period ended is 31 May. The VAT liability for the year ended 31 May 20X1 is £6,980 and for the year ended 31 May 20X2 is £7,211.

(i) What monthly payments on account should the business make for the year ended 31 May 20X2?

698

(ii) What is the balancing payment for the year ended 31 May 20X2?

929

TASK 1.5

(a)   For each of the following businesses, indicate whether they can correct their (non deliberate) errors on their next VAT return or whether they are required to make separate disclosure (tick the appropriate box).

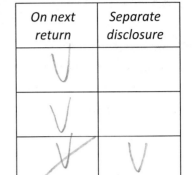

	On next return	Separate disclosure
(i) A business with a net error of £15,552 and a turnover of £2,800,000.	✓	
(ii) A business with a net error of £8,032 and a turnover of £58,000.	✓	
(iii) A business with a net error of £12,156 and a turnover of £810,000.	✗	✓

(b)   (i)   Joe starts his business on 1 June 20X1. He has taxable supplies of £7,800 per month.

When does he need to notify HMRC?

Day _30_ Month _4_ Year _X2_.

(ii)   What date will he be registered from?

Day _1_ Month _5_ Year _X2_

SECTION 2

TASK 2.1

You have been given the following information about the business transactions of X Ltd for the quarter ended 31 December 20X3.

	£
Sales of standard rated items	250,000 — 41 666'66
Purchases of standard rated goods	162,000
Purchases of zero rated goods	21,500

You are also told that

1   There is an 8 month old bad debt on a sales invoice for £1,250 including VAT and a 5 month old bad debt on a sales invoice for £1,212 excluding VAT. These have both been written off in the accounts

2   A non deliberate error was made in the previous return. Output tax was understated by £3,200.12.

3   All figures are VAT inclusive unless told otherwise.

(a)   Calculate the figure to be claimed for bad debt relief. £...208.33...

(b)   Calculate the VAT due on sales and other outputs (Box 1). £...44 866,79...

(c)   Calculate the VAT reclaimed in the period on purchases and other inputs (Box 4).
£...27 008.33...

TASK 2.2

The following has been extracted from the company's ledgers for the quarter ended 31 March 20X1:

Sales: UK

Date		£.pp
31/01/20X1	Sales day-book	212,630.00
28/02/20X1	Sales day-book	305,000.00
31/03/20X1	Sales day-book	286,250.00

803 880

Sales: Export EU (VAT registered businesses)

Date		£.pp
31/01/20X1	Sales day-book	25,150.00
28/02/20X1	Sales day-book	14,920.00
31/03/20X1	Sales day-book	19,879.00

59949

Sales: Export non-EU

Date		£.pp
31/01/20X1	Sales day-book	15,600.00
28/02/20X1	Sales day-book	9,820.00
31/03/20X1	Sales day-book	16,780.00

42200

Purchases: UK

Date		£.pp
31/01/20X1	Purchases day-book	68,350.00
28/02/20X1	Purchases day-book	75,213.00
31/03/20X1	Purchases day-book	71,456.00

2|5019

Output VAT

Date		£.pp
31/01/20X1	Sales day-book	42,526.00
28/02/20X1	Sales day-book	61,000.00
31/03/20X1	Sales day-book	57,250.00

160776

Input VAT

Date		£.pp
31/01/20X1	Purchases day-book	13,670.00
28/02/20X1	Purchases day-book	15,042.60
31/03/20X1	Purchases day-book	14,291.20

45003.8

- VAT returns are completed quarterly.
- Today's date is 18 April 20X1.

Complete Boxes 1 to 9 of the VAT return for the quarter ended 31 March 20X1.

43003.8

		£
VAT due in this period on **sales** and other outputs	**Box 1**	160.776
VAT due in this period on **acquisitions** from other **EC Member States**	**Box 2**	0
Total VAT due (**the sum of boxes 1 and 2**)	**Box 3**	160 776
VAT reclaimed in the period on **purchases** and other inputs, including acquisitions from the EC	**Box 4**	43003.8
Net VAT to be paid to HM Revenue & Customs or reclaimed by you (**Difference between boxes 3 and 4**)	**Box 5**	117772.2
Total value of **sales** and all other outputs excluding any VAT. **Include your box 8 figure**	**Box 6**	906029
Total value of purchases and all other inputs excluding any VAT. **Include your box 9 figure**	**Box 7**	215019
Total value of all **supplies** of goods and related costs, excluding any VAT, to other **EC Member States**	**Box 8**	59949
Total value of all **acquisitions** of goods and related costs, excluding any VAT, from other **EC Member States**	**Box 9**	0

TASK 2.3

You are an accounting technician. The company financial accountant has asked you to deal with the VAT return for the quarter ended 30 June 20X5.

The Box 5 figure from the VAT return you have just completed is £11,657.42 (positive).

Today's date is 16 July 20X5.

Complete the following email to the financial accountant advising him of the amount of VAT that will be paid or received and the date due.

To: F. A.

From: _A O._

Date: 16 July 20X5

Subject: VAT return

Please be advised that I have just completed the VAT return for the quarter ended (30-6-X5).

The amount of VAT **(payable/receivable)** will be £ (11,652.42).

This will be **(paid electronically by** 7-8   ) / **(received directly into our bank account)**

Kind regards

Section 4

MOCK ASSESSMENT ANSWERS

SECTION 1

TASK 1.1

	True	False
A business has an expected turnover for the next 12 months of £85,000 but they sell goods that are zero-rated so they cannot register for VAT.		√
A business has prepared their VAT return for the quarter ended 31 March 20X2. They must pay by electronic transfer by 30 April 20X2.		√
Tax evasion is illegal.	√	

Tutorial note

*Traders who make zero rated supplies are making taxable supplies and **can** register for VAT.*

Payments are due 1 month and 7 days after the end of the VAT quarter with an extra 3 bank working days if paying by direct debit.

TASK 1.2

(a)   The correct answer is B.

£106.40 (£560 × 95% × 20%)

Tutorial note

VAT is always calculated on the lowest amount receivable regards of whether the discount is actually taken or not. The lowest amount receivable is £560 less a 5% discount = £532

(b)   The answer is C.

The amount payable will decrease by £8. The VAT on the credit note is £8 (£40 x 20%) and this will reduce the amount the business needs to pay HMRC. This has the same effect as VAT on a purchase.

TASK 1.3

(a)

Item	Net £	VAT £	Gross £	Reclaim?
Motor car	2,500.00	500.00	3,000.00	X
Stationery	25.00	5.00	30.00	√
Fixtures and fittings	1,212.00	242.40	1,454.40	√
Staff entertaining	250.00	50.00	300.00	√
Printer	65.00	13.00	78.00	√

(b)   The answer is A.

Tutorial note

The basic tax point is the date of delivery of goods or the date of performance of services.

However, if goods or services are paid for in advance or a tax invoice is issued in advance, the date of payment or the invoice date becomes the tax point date.

TASK 1.4

(a)   The answer is C.

Tutorial note

The annual accounting scheme is not useful for businesses that are experiencing lower turnover than the previous year as the liability is based on the previous year's turnover not this year.

For repayment businesses, they would have to wait longer for their refund if they are only completing one return per annum.

(b)   (i)   The answer is £698 (£6,980 × 10%).

The POA's are always based on the previous year's VAT liability.

(ii)   The answer is £929.

The POA's are paid at the end of months 4 – 12 so there are nine instalments.

(9 months × £698) = £6,282 paid during the year.

This year's liability is £7,211 so the difference is the balancing payment

i.e. (£7,211 – £6,282) = £929

TASK 1.5

(a)

	On next return	Separate disclosure
(i) A business with a net error of £15,552 and a turnover of £2,800,000.	√	
(ii) A business with a net error of £8,032 and a turnover of £58,000.	√	
(iii) A business with a net error of £12,156 and a turnover of £810,000.		√

Tutorial note

When a trader discovers a VAT error they must inform HMRC. If the net error is less than a certain limit and is not deliberate, it can be included on the next VAT return. If not, it must be disclosed separately on Form VAT 652 or in a letter.

The limit operates as follows:

Net errors up to £10,000 can always be included on the next VAT return.

Net errors above £50,000 must always be separately disclosed.

Errors between these limits can be included on the next VAT return if they are no more than 1% of turnover (specifically the figure in Box 6 of the return.

(b) (i) 30 April 20X2.

The trader exceeds the registration limit after 10 months trading – by the end of March 20X2. He must notify HMRC by 30 days after exceeding the threshold.

(ii) 1 May 20X2

SECTION 2

TASK 2.1

(a) Bad debt relief is £208.33 (£1,250 × 20/120)

(b) VAT due on sales and other outputs £44,866.78 (W1)

(c) VAT reclaimed on purchases and other inputs £27,208.33 (W2)

Workings

(W1) **Box 1**

		£.pp
VAT on standard rated sales	(£250,000 × 20/120)	41,666.66
VAT error		3,200.12
		44,866.78

(W2) **Box 4**

	£.pp
VAT on purchases of standard rated goods (£162,000 × 20/120)	27,000.00
Bad debt relief	208.33
	27,208.33

Tutorial note

There has to be at least 6 months since the due date for payment of the invoice before the VAT can be reclaimed. Therefore the VAT on the 5 month old invoice cannot be reclaimed until next quarter.

When a trader discovers a VAT error they must inform HMRC. If the net error is less than a certain limit and is not deliberate, it can be included on the next VAT return. If not, it must be disclosed separately on Form VAT 652 or in a letter.

The limit operates as follows:

* *Net errors up to £10,000 can always be included on the next VAT return.*

* *Net errors above £50,000 must always be separately disclosed.*

Errors between these limits can be included on the next VAT return if they are no more than 1% of turnover (specifically the figure in Box 6 of the return).

TASK 2.2

VAT return for the quarter ended 31 March 20X1

		£
VAT due in this period on **sales** and other outputs	Box 1	160,776.00
VAT due in this period on **acquisitions** from other **EC Member States**	Box 2	0.00
Total VAT due (**the sum of boxes 1 and 2**)	Box 3	160,776.00
VAT reclaimed in the period on **purchases** and other inputs, including acquisitions from the EC	Box 4	43,003.80
Net VAT to be paid to HM Revenue & Customs or reclaimed by you (**Difference between boxes 3 and 4**)	Box 5	117,772.20
Total value of **sales** and all other outputs excluding any VAT. **Include your box 8 figure**	Box 6	906,029
Total value of purchases and all other inputs excluding any VAT. **Include your box 9 figure**	Box 7	215,019
Total value of all **supplies** of goods and related costs, excluding any VAT, to other **EC Member States**	Box 8	59,949
Total value of all **acquisitions** of goods and related costs, excluding any VAT, from other **EC Member States**	Box 9	0

Workings

	£.pp
Box 1 – Output tax	
31/01/X1	42,526.00
28/02/X1	61,000.00
31/03/X1	57,250.00
	————
	160,776.00
	————

	£.pp
Box 4 – Input tax	
31/01/X1	13,670.00
28/02/X1	15,042.60
31/03/X1	14,291.20
	43,003.80

	£
Box 6 – Total outputs	
UK sales (£212,630 + £305,000 + £286,250)	803,880
EC sales (£25,150 + £14,920 + £19,879)	59,949
Non EC sales (£15,600 + £9,820 + £16,780)	42,200
	906,029

Box 7 – Total inputs	
31/01/X1	68,350
28/02/X1	75,213
31/03/X1	71,456
	215,019

Box 8 – EC Sales	
31/01/11	25,150
28/02/11	14,920
31/03/11	19,879
	59,949

Tutorial note

Export sales are dealt with as follows:

Sales to registered businesses in the EU are zero rated so there is no output VAT to include in Box 1. The sales are part of the total outputs included in Box 6 and are also entered in Box 8.

Sales to non registered customers in the EU are treated just like normal UK sales and are not included in Box 8.

Sales to customers outside the EU are zero rated and they only appear on the VAT return as part of the outputs in Box 6.

TASK 2.3

E mail to Financial Accountant

To:	**Financial Accountant**
From:	**Accounting Technician**
Date:	**16 July 20X5**
Subject:	**VAT return**

Please be advised that I have just completed the VAT return for the quarter ended **30 June 20X5.**

The amount of VAT **payable** will be **£11,657.42.**

This will be **paid electronically by 7 August 20X5.**

Kind regards